american baby books

The American Baby Handbook

Published by American Baby Books
Wauwatosa, WI 53226

ISBN 0-940212-02-1
Copyright © MCMLXXXI by American Baby Books
All rights reserved.
Published by American Baby Books
Wauwatosa, WI 53226
Printed and bound in U.S.A.
Published simultaneously in Canada.

Introduction

Being a parent is one of life's most rewarding experiences. To help make the challenges of raising your children a little easier, we've compiled *The American Baby Handbook*. The handbook, which consists of articles from *American Baby* Magazine, contains an overview of everything you need to know about parenting—from diapering and feeding how-tos to coping with sibling rivalry. There's expert advice from *American Baby's* staff of contributing medical experts and commonsense suggestions from experienced parents. In addition to comprehensive information about labor and delivery, you'll find articles about controversial subjects like spanking, and working mothers.

The handbook is divided into five chapters to make it easy for you to use as a reference guide. We hope that you'll refer to the handbook many times for information and for moral support to help guide you along the sometimes rocky road of parenthood.

The Editors
American Baby Magazine

Table of Contents

Chapter 1
Pregnancy and Childbirth

Labor And Delivery Guide, Part 1

Labor. It means hard work, and the labor associated with childbirth is no exception.

What happens in labor? What does it feel like? What happens in the hospital? All these and many other questions will be answered in this two-part series on labor and delivery, prepared by the editors of American Baby *Magazine, with photographs by the Maternity Center Association.*

It is our hope that by describing in detail what happens during labor and delivery, the "mystique" of pain and fear that surrounds the entire process will be at least partially dissolved.

Labor is the term given to the entire process of bringing the baby into the world. The course of labor and the expulsion of the fetus are usually considered in three separate stages. For purposes of this article, we will focus on the first stage—from the onset of labor to full dilation of the cervix. Stage II begins when the cervix is completely dilated and ends with the birth of the baby. Stage III is from the completion of delivery of the baby to completion of delivery of the afterbirth, or placenta.

First-stage labor is further broken down into three separate categories, and it will help you to know what they are so that you will know approximately how close you are to actual delivery. These three categories are early labor, active labor, and transition labor.

But before we discuss the progress of labor, it would help to understand what is happening inside of you and the functions of some of the major organs and muscles used during pregnancy and birth.

The Body During Pregnancy

The *uterus* (womb) is a hollow organ that measures about two inches by four inches. By the end of pregnancy, it measures about 10 inches by 14 inches. In volume its capacity increases about 500 times; in weight it grows from about 1-1/2 ounces to almost 30 ounces. The muscle fibers that make up the uterus grow to 10 times their original thickness. After pregnancy the uterus returns to approximately its size before pregnancy.

The uterus is made up of the cervix—the mouth or opening—which is long and thick during pregnancy, and the fundus (upper uterine segment), which grows and thins out with pregnancy. The upper segment contracts and retracts. The cervix becomes softer and thinner and dilates as it is pulled upward around the baby's head during labor.

The uterus is one of the strongest muscles in the body. During the height of a uterine contraction, the pressures created are considerable. Yet this muscle contracts regularly throughout a woman's life. Though most women are not aware of this, the contractions may be noticed as pains associated with the menstrual period.

Throughout pregnancy the uterus contracts at slightly irregular intervals, about every 15 or 20 minutes and lasting for about 25 seconds. They may be felt as a tightening of the abdomen, but they are not painful. Many years ago these contractions were described by Braxton Hicks and have since become known as Braxton-Hicks contractions. What they do is exercise the uterus and prepare it for functioning during actual labor. These contractions do not progress (get closer together), but they are useful in assisting the circulation of maternal blood to the placenta.

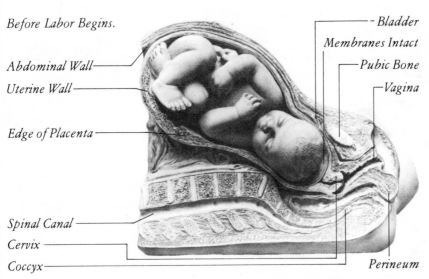

Before Labor Begins.

Abdominal Wall

Uterine Wall

Edge of Placenta

Spinal Canal

Cervix

Coccyx

Bladder

Membranes Intact

Pubic Bone

Vagina

Perineum

This is a typical position. The baby faces the right side of his mother with his arms and legs flexed. He has descended slightly into the pelvis, and his head is crowding the pelvic organs. He looks big in relation to the birth canal (vagina), but they adjust to each other as labor progresses.

Labor Has Begun.

Rectum —

Cervix —

The baby's position changes gradually to accommodate the largest diameters of his body to the largest diameters of the pelvis. As he descends, his head becomes more flexed. There is increased crowding of the mother's bladder and rectum. The cervix is almost completely thinned out and has not begun to dilate.

Second Stage Begins.   ┌Vagina

Membranes Bulging —

During a contraction, the baby is driven in the direction of the birth canal. The cervix is now open enough to permit the baby to begin his passage through the vagina. His face is turning farther toward his mother's back. As he moves down, pressure increases on the mother's bladder and rectum. The membranes are still intact and bulging in front of the baby's head.

Crowning of the Head.

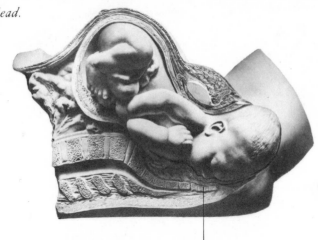

Coccyx Bent Back —

Labor is almost over. The baby is being pushed down through the birth canal by the uterine contractions and the mother's bearing down. The crown of his head can be seen at the outlet of the vagina. His face is completely turned toward his mother's back.

Second Stage Progressing.

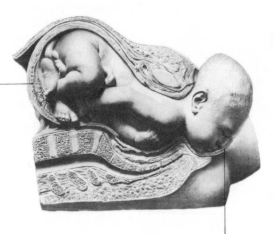

Uterine Wall —

Perineum —

As labor continues, the baby's head emerges. The perineum is shrinking and thickening. The baby's body continues to turn. The thickening wall of the uterus fits cap-shape over his buttocks.

Signs Of Approaching Labor

Toward the end of pregnancy, these contractions become stronger and more regular. Now it is time to ask the question, "When does labor really begin?" Since each labor is unique, it is almost impossible to give a general answer. But there are three distinctive signs that labor is about to begin, and most women will recognize one or all of them, though not necessarily in this order.

The *first sign* is the onset of regular, progressive uterine contractions, occurring every 5 to 20 minutes and lasting from about 45 seconds to a minute. They are uncomfortable but not necessarily painful. They are accompanied by a definite hardening of the uterus, which can easily be felt by placing your hand on your abdomen.

The *second sign* is rupture of the membranes or the "bag of waters." Also called the "forewaters," this is a quantity of liquid that lies in front of the baby's head and is held within the uterus by intact membranes. When these membranes rupture, it is a sign to call your doctor. Rupture may occur slowly by leaking or in a gush. The fluid is clear and sweet-smelling. But the rupture will not hurt as there are no nerves in the membranes. For many women, rupture does not occur until early or late in labor, and in this case, the doctor will do it.

A *third sign* is the passage of a small amount of blood-stained mucus or brownish blood called the "show" or "bloody show." Sometimes you will find this on your underclothes. It is the mucus plug that has been formed during pregnancy to close off the cervix. The mucus plug keeps the uterus free from germs and allows you to swim and have intercourse during pregnancy without fear of infection. Many women never experience this "show" while others have an increasing amount all through the first stage of labor and some have it as early as two weeks before the onset of labor.

Other common signs of approaching labor are diarrhea, backache, decreased movement of the baby, an increase in Braxton-Hicks contractions, and an increased desire to clean everything in sight! This last so-called "nesting instinct" often occurs on the very day labor begins.

What Happens During Labor

What will labor feel like? No one can answer this question for you because there are so many variables that affect the length of labor and what it feels like. Among them are the pain threshold of the mother, the preparation she has had for labor and delivery, the position and size of the baby, and how quickly the baby moves through the birth canal. However, there are some descriptions of labor that will prove useful.

First-stage labor has three parts: early labor, active labor, and transition. Early labor is concerned with opening up the mouth of the uterus (the cervix). Before labor begins, the wall of the uterus is thin. The cervical canal is narrow, and the membranes are still intact. Now, the bands of longitudinal muscle fiber in the main part of the uterus are contracting and thus gradually drawing up, thinning, and opening the walls of the cervix. The cervical canal thus gets shorter until the cervix is of the same thickness as the uterine wall. This process of shortening the length of the cervical canal and taking it up into the uterus is known as *effacement,* or "taking up of the cervix." (It may help you to visualize a wine bottle with a long, thick neck. Cutting off the neck would be the equivalent of effacement.) Effacement is measured in percentages, from 0-100 percent, so if you are 80 percent effaced, that means the opening of your cervix is almost totally thinned out.

Once the cervix is effaced, the force of uterine contractions begins to dilate the cervix, although effacement and dilation may occur simultaneously. *Dilation* (or dilatation) is the term used to refer to the size of the round opening of the cervix. It is measured in centimeters, sometimes in finger widths. Full dilation is 10 centimeters, or five finger widths.

Dilation is slow during the early first part of labor. It usually takes much longer to go from one to three fingers dilation than it does to go from three fingers to full dilation.

Some mothers are already partially effaced and one or two fingers dilated when they start labor. The process of dilation has begun without their being aware of it.

Timing The Contractions

Once labor is really under way, the contractions will become stronger and closer together. Many women describe them as moving like waves, gathering in the distance, rising, breaking, and falling on the shore. The pressure in the uterus is rising slowly and increasing in power until it reaches a maximum where there is a crest or plateau, which lasts for about 30 to 50 seconds and then disappears rapidly. When it is over, you feel nothing until the next contraction, which may be anywhere from 20 to five minutes away. It varies for every woman. What you will feel is a gradual tightening of the uterine muscles and a discomfort or a gripping sensation around the pelvis and a nagging backache.

As the cervix continues to dilate, the strength and frequency of the contractions gradually increase. Now the discomfort is felt over the whole of the uterus. The cervix is dilated three centimeters, and the longest part of labor is over. Early labor is often the most easily handled and the least uncomfortable. But since it may take up to six hours or more, most women stay home until this stage is over. Once you are in the hospital, you are a patient, confined to a room and a bed, and if you arrive there too early, you may be sent home.

Most women are told to call their doctor when their contractions are five minutes apart and have been that way for a full hour, or if the membranes rupture. If you are comfortable, be sure to indicate this to your doctor, and he may let you remain home a while longer, depending on your individual pregnancy. If there is any bleeding or one prolonged contraction, call your doctor. These are signs to leave immediately for the hospital.

Hospital Procedures

Once in the hospital, you will have a vaginal examination, and depending on hospital policy, a physical examination and medical history. If you have arrived too early and are discharged, you may have to pay a fee. But if you are in active labor, you will be admitted and asked to pay part or all of the agreed-upon costs.

You will be taken to a labor room and given a partial shave on either side of the pubic area to keep it clean. (Nowadays in most hospitals, a complete pubic area shave is not done.)

You may or may not be given an enema upon admission to the hospital. Once labor begins, digestion stops, and many women have diarrhea in early labor. If this happens to you, be sure to tell your doctor.

Once labor has started, don't eat. Drink only black tea or eat some jello. You don't want to feel nauseous during the later stages of labor. In the hospital you'll be given only ice chips.

In most hospitals today, you will also be monitored—both for your baby's heart (an electrical impulse) and for your uterine contractions (a mechanical impulse). The monitor gives a continuous picture of the fetal environment. It is attached to you by way of two belts: one is placed just above the pubic hairline to monitor the baby's heart, and another is placed just below your navel to check the uterine contractions. This monitoring will be done from the time you enter the hospital to the time your baby is born. The machine, mounted on a movable table, goes with you from labor room to delivery room. Most hospitals routinely use fetal heart monitoring, and if you are lucky enough to also have the uterine contraction monitoring, you can see the contraction coming before you actually feel it and can prepare for it. (If the membranes have ruptured, you may have an internal fetal monitor for the baby's heart. A wire, inserted through the vagina, is attached to the baby's head and gives a complete picture.)

The Final Stages Before Delivery

Active labor is the stage when the cervix dilates from three to seven centimeters. By the time you are six centimeters dilated, the contractions may be very strong and will gradually increase in frequency until they are occurring every two to three minutes and lasting about 60 seconds. You may feel a definite and uncomfortable rise of pressure and tension and then a gradual lessening until the contraction is over. You may also feel you have to defecate even though in early labor digestion stopped and you may have had diarrhea. This is a positive sign, indicating that baby's head is on the rectum, and the end is near.

From eight to ten centimeters is the hardest and shortest part of labor. This stage is called *transition*, and for most women, this is what gives the whole experience a bad name. It is discouraging and often considered the most painful part of labor. The closer you get to this stage, the more intense will be your contractions, lasting for 90 seconds and about one minute apart, and the more help you will need to cope with them. But this stage only lasts between 20 and 45 minutes. Some common signs of transition are: irritability, rectal pressure, premature urge to push, bloody show, shaking and chills and / or nausea, vomiting, leg cramps, perspiration, and discouragement. (If these signs do not occur during transition, the cold and shaking can occur after delivery of the placenta. It can be quite overwhelming, but it passes quickly.)

Suddenly, just when you think that you can't go on, you will feel an entirely different sensation. It is hard to describe, but it will be different from any previous feeling of contractions. You will feel a pressure in the pelvis and an almost uncontrollable desire to push or bear down. But unless the doctor says you are a full 10 centimeters dilated, you must not push or you could tear your cervix. Once you are fully dilated, the cervix is completely open and becomes part of the uterus. Uterus, cervix, and vagina then form one canal for the baby to pass through.

By the combined force of your pushing with the diaphragm and abdominal muscles, and the uterine contractions, the baby's head descends and stretches the pelvic floor so that it comes into contact with the muscular outlet of the pelvis, known as the perineum. There is pressure in the rectum and stretching of the ligaments of the coccyx (tailbone). As the perineum is slowly distended, there may be some discomfort in the back, almost like a tearing sensation, as if everything were splitting wide open. Actual tearing does not occur because the vaginal opening can stretch to wide proportions.

With the onset of pushing, delivery of the baby (second-stage labor) has begun, and in 20 to 90 minutes your baby will be born. The entire first stage may take anywhere from 10 to 12 hours for a first-time mother. For a second-time mother, the time is between five and six hours.

Presentation Of The Baby

The baby, before labor begins, has descended slightly into the pelvis, and his head is crowding the pelvic organs. As labor begins and progresses, his position gradually changes to accommodate the largest diameters of the body to the largest diameters of the pelvis. As he descends, he rotates, and there is increased crowding of the mother's bladder and rectum.

The baby's skull is not hard bone all over, and his skull bones have not yet grown together. There are soft spots, or fontanels, at the front and back of the head, with a narrow gap connecting the two. During the second stage of labor, the skull is molded by overlapping of the bones. By internal examination the doctor can feel these fontanels through the dilating cervix and can determine which way the baby's head is lying.

The presentation of the baby is usually by the back of the head (vertex), though the face, brow, or breech (buttocks) can present. The most common and most favorable way for the baby to present is with his head down, the nose facing the mother's back, with the back part of his skull (the occiput) toward the mother's front. The baby can be lying on the left side (in medical terms called left occiput anterior or L.O.A.) or on the right side (right occiput anterior R.O.A.). The left position is the more common of these and is an efficient way for the baby to move through the birth canal.

Some babies lie in the posterior position, facing either right or left, and the occiput is toward the mother's back (called right occiput posterior R.O.P., or left occiput posterior L.O.P.). These positions are less favorable because the baby will try to turn around during labor in order to be born facing the mother's back. Labor will be longer and more uncomfortable and will create more severe backache pains, which increase in intensity during contractions, then lessen, but don't go away totally. Occasionally the baby begins to rotate but gets stuck in a transverse (across) position, and if he remains in this posterior position, help from the doctor is needed.

In a face presentation (very rare), the baby's head is not flexed onto his chest as it usually is, and unless his head is small, labor may be slower and help may be needed with delivery. Brow presentation is also very rare.

The breech (buttocks down or feet first) presentation occurs in about three percent of deliveries. This, too, can cause a longer labor with contractions felt in the back.

The dangers in breech births are multiple. The baby could take its first breath as soon as the buttocks are born and the head is still inside, and swallow fluid.

If the delivery of the head is prolonged, the umbilical cord could be caught between the baby's head and the mother's pelvis, decreasing the flow of oxygen to the baby. The doctor may use forceps for the head or may insert a finger into the birth canal to clear a passageway for air to reach the baby's face. A Cesarean section is often performed in breech births for fetal safety.

The baby's head can be seen at the entrance to the vagina when it begins to distend the perineum. Since it is the crown of the head that will first be visible, this moment is known as "the crowning of the baby's head." At this point—or in some cases, when the doctor can actually see the baby's hair—you will be moved into the delivery room. This is particularly true for first babies; for second, the move takes place earlier—when the cervix has reached full dilation. In minutes your baby will be fully delivered.

You will be transferred to a delivery table with legs put in stirrups, then prepped and draped. The doctor may perform an episiotomy to enlarge the vaginal opening and to ease the delivery of the baby's head. An episiotomy is an incision of the perineum between the vagina and the anus. A local anesthesia is used so it will not hurt.

Methods Of Pain Relief

There are roughly two sides to the issue of pain: one is that labor pains are the most excruciating that a woman will ever experience. The other view is that with proper preparation for childbirth, pain and discomfort can be controlled and greatly reduced.

We stand somewhere in between. When you consider what the body has to go through to help deliver the child, it would be naive to think that this wouldn't cause discomfort. In fact, it hurts, and depending on the woman and a number of factors, it may hurt a little or a lot. But it is true that with proper preparation in a prenatal class, the experience can be less painful.

There are essentially four ways to help diminish, control, alleviate, or completely eliminate pain and discomfort during labor. This discussion is not meant to be an exhaustive one but rather a brief description of the methods and some of the advantages and disadvantages of each.

1) Psychological Pain Relief. Psychoprophylaxis (or prepared childbirth) is a method of pain relief by conditioned reflex. As taught by the French obstetrician Fernand Lamaze and his advocates, the approach is twofold: first, the mother learns breathing exercises to use during labor and delivery, which distract her from conscious awareness of pain and help her to relax. Secondly, the mother is educated about what to expect during labor and delivery, and this helps reduce the fear and anxiety that can intensify pain. By attending six classes with her husband eight weeks before her due date, she becomes prepared for the experience of labor and delivery.

The advantage of this method is that it is educational. Regardless of which method or combination of pain-relief methods you finally use in the labor room, there is no substitute for knowing ahead of time what to expect. Every couple should take these classes, whether they plan to go through with the breathing exercises or not. Sharing the birth experience as a couple is described by many as one of life's most exciting moments. Finally, the Lamaze teaching discourages using drugs and encourages the mother to be fully awake when the baby is delivered. Today in most hospitals, parents are told to go through the Lamaze training, and many of the classes are given in conjunction with the hospital.

Another variation of this method is called "natural childbirth" and was developed by Dr. Grantly Dick-Read before the Lamaze method. The course emphasis is slightly different, but the underlying point is the same—fear and tension lead to pain in labor, and all can be eliminated with proper knowledge and conditioning.

2) *Drugs.* There are many drugs and combinations of drugs used today to alleviate labor pains. They are given by hypodermic injection directly into a vein or muscle. We can't list all of them here, but a definition of certain terms will help clear up confusion about which drug and which method might be used. An *analgesic* is a drug that relieves or diminishes the sense of pain. Aspirin, for example, is a mild analgesic.

The analgesics used today (Demerol and morphine) can lessen your perception of pain, thereby increasing your pain threshold. They are often used in combination with *tranquilizers* (such as Phenergan, Valium, Sparine, and Vistaril), which enhance the analgesic effect of the drugs and lessen the total amount given. They may reduce anxiety and may induce drowsiness and loss of concentration.

These drugs are central nervous system depressants, depressing not only the sensation of pain but other nervous mechanisms, including breathing. The majority of drugs administered during labor will slow the progress of labor and will cross the placenta and therefore enter the baby's circulation, where they will exert an effect similar to that which is exerted on the mother. No matter by what route they have been given, they will gain access to her blood and therefore to her baby's. For this reason doctors and childbirth educators today caution against the excessive use of drugs. We simply don't know what effects they may have on the fetus. The baby may be drowsy at birth, though he will recover quickly. But the final evidence on drugs is not yet in, and you should be aware of the possible hazards and/or the need for drugs used during labor and discuss this with your doctor.

3) *Anesthesia.* An *anesthetic* obliterates all sensation, either through the production of transitory unconsciousness (general anesthetic) or by temporarily interrupting the pathway by which sensory nerves communicate pain to the brain (called conduction or regional anesthesia).

Regional anesthetics are widely used in labor at varying stages of cervical dilation. Essentially, they anesthetize the nerves in a specific area of the body by interrupting the path from the area of pain stimulus to the brain. Since they act locally, little of the anesthesia is absorbed into the mother's bloodstream, and only small amounts cross the placenta. Still there are cautions against the use of some of these methods, and an anesthesiologist should be present to administer the medication.

There is a high degree of pain relief with these methods, although you will still feel the pressure of the contractions. Common side effects include slowing of contractions, mild hypotension (lowering of blood pressure), and a loss of the bearing down reflex. Since abdominal muscles are affected, a forceps delivery may be indicated.

The forms of *conduction blocks* (as they are called) are named for the location where they are given. A *caudal block* is given in the space at the base of the back (sacral canal). It may be given in one shot, or it may be administered through a catheter (tube), which is introduced into the lower back, and the anesthetic is then injected through the catheter. If needed, additional amounts are given as soon as the numbness wears off.

Epidural anesthesia is injected by an anesthesiologist between two vertebrae in the lower back—into the extradural space outside of the spinal canal—and causes numbness from the navel to the toe area. It slows the progress of labor and sometimes causes a slight drop in blood pressure. If a catheter is used, additional medication can be given as the effects wear off, but you can be up immediately after delivery.

A *paracervical* block is the injection of anesthesia by your obstetrician on either side of the cervix and the lower lateral borders of the uterus. A paracervical block provides anesthesia during labor but doesn't numb the perineal area. Therefore, if an episiotomy is performed, local anesthesia is also necessary. A *pudendal* block anesthetizes the nerve fibers in the external organs—the perineum, vagina, and the entrance to the vagina (vulva). There can be a loss of the bearing down reflex if given too soon.

A *spinal* is a one-shot injection of medication into the spinal column that numbs the body from below the breasts to the toes and allows you to be awake during delivery. It may be used for a Cesarean section. After delivery 20 percent of women develop spinal headaches and must stay flat for 18 to 24 hours.

A *saddle block* is a low spinal administered by your obstetrician when you are fully dilated. It numbs the area where you would sit if in a saddle, and the position for administration is most uncomfortable. A forceps delivery is indicated, and the side effects are the same as from a spinal.

Local anesthesia is an injection into the perineum that provides a numbing effect before an episiotomy is performed. It doesn't interfere with pushing and has no known side effects.

General anesthesia is the method of putting the mother completely to sleep and is done either by inhalation of nitrous oxide or ether, or by intravenous sodium pentothal. The whole body is affected, creating temporary but complete unconsciousness.

This method is not used very often today because of the potential hazards to both mother and baby. The anesthetics will pass across the placenta into the baby's circulation and may make him sleepy, though with careful handling he will be fine. If this method is used, it is usually not until very late in labor. (Many women argue that this is when pain relief is least needed.) But sometimes the method is needed, as in the case of an emergency Cesarean section.

There is growing evidence about risks in each of the above methods, the most common being a sudden drop in the mother's blood pressure that can jeopardize her welfare and the baby's. Again, ask your doctor what he might use and when.

The important issue here is not which method or combination of methods you use to deliver your baby, but the baby itself. Nothing should overshadow the experience of having the baby. Your doctor is there to offer you help if you're having trouble, but to keep the right perspective, remember why you're really there—to deliver a healthy baby.

Quick Dictionary Of Terms

analgesic—a drug that relieves or diminishes sense of pain

anesthetic—a substance that obliterates all sensation, either through transitory unconsciousness, or by temporarily interrupting the path between sensory nerves and brain

bag of waters—(also called forewaters)—liquid that lies in front of baby's head and is held intact by uterine membranes

birth canal—space through which the baby moves in order to be born; formed by uterus, cervix, and the vagina

Braxton-Hicks contractions—preliminary, painless contractions

cervix—mouth of the uterus

dilation—(or dilatation)—the size of the round opening of the cervix; measured in centimeters or finger widths

effacement—process of thinning or "taking up" the cervix

first-stage labor—from the onset of labor to full dilation of the cervix

occiput—back part of the baby's skull

psychoprophylaxis—method of pain relief by conditioned reflex; the basis for prepared childbirth

second-stage labor—from full dilation of the cervix to birth of the baby

show—(or bloody show)—blood-stained mucus from the plug that has been at the mouth of the cervix; often a sign of beginning labor

third-stage labor—from completion of baby's delivery to completion of delivery of the afterbirth

transition—labor from eight to ten centimeters dilation; often considered the hardest part of labor

uterus—(or womb)—hollow organ that expands to house the baby

Labor And Delivery Guide, Part 2

In Part One of our Labor and Delivery Guide, *we reviewed the first signs and stages of labor and discussed the physical changes that must occur before the baby can be born. Here we focus on the second and third stages of labor—the delivery of the baby and the placenta —and the first few days postpartum.*

If you listened to ten mothers describing their own labor and delivery, you would hear ten different versions of what childbirth is "really" like. Here, we describe a so-called "average" childbirth. We hope this helps prepare you for the unique experience of the birth of your own baby.

The word *delivery* comes from the Latin *de* (from) and *liber* (free). At this point in your labor, the baby is working his way down the birth canal so that his "delivery" from the womb is imminent.

During the *transition* stage, you may have experienced an urge to push or bear down. Since your cervix was not fully dilated, the doctor/nurse encouraged you not to push and advised you to pant lightly and "blow out" continuously when you felt the urge to push. (Pushing prematurely will tire you out by expending unnecessary energy and possibly tear your cervix.) The desire to push may be sudden and overwhelming. Some women never feel this pressure and must follow the doctor's direction to bear down.

The onset of pushing marks the beginning of the *second stage of labor.* For the primapara (woman giving birth for the first time) delivery will begin in the labor room. At full dilation the doctor will tell you that you may push when you feel the urge. With each contraction your baby's head is moving lower, aided by your bearing down. Many women describe the second stage as the "best" part of labor, since they can take an active part in their child's birth by bearing down at the appropriate time.

The primapara must push the baby from full dilation to the opening of the vagina (approximately four inches). This may take as little as 20 minutes or as long as an hour and 15 minutes. When a portion of the baby's head—about the size of a quarter—is visible at the opening of the vagina, you will be transferred to the delivery room. Multiparas (women who have previously given birth) will go to the delivery room as soon as they are fully dilated. This is because their pelvic floor muscles have been previously stretched, and the descent of the baby will be more rapid.

The descent of the baby is aided by your bearing down with the diaphragm and abdominal muscles. The head will move forward with each contraction and recede slightly at the end of the contraction when downward pressure is no longer being directed.

The Delivery Room

The delivery room is really a fully-equipped operating room with table, anesthesia machine, infant-resuscitation machine, and other items that may be needed. If you have had a hospital tour beforehand (usually included in childbirth preparation classes), the room and equipment will seem not ominous, but reassuring.

The most common delivery position is called *lithotomy:* you will be lying on your back with two pillows behind your head and shoulders; your legs will be simultaneously placed in stirrups. The position is similar to that used during a gynecological exam except that the stirrups support the back of the thighs and legs instead of just the feet. Stirrups can be adjusted to make you comfortable, and they may make pushing a bit easier as you are no longer supporting the full weight of your legs.

Some hospitals are experimenting with a French labor-delivery bed that can be easily adapted to delivery requirements. The laboring woman can thus remain in the same bed (and room) for the entire childbirth process.

After your legs are placed in the stirrups, your hands will be placed on a metal pistol grip on either side of the delivery table to assist you in lifting yourself up during the expulsion of the baby. Wrist straps are still used on occasion. They prevent you from accidentally touching the sterile drapes used during delivery. If you are awake and in control of your contractions, wrist straps are not indicated. The doctor will wash you with a disinfectant (prep) and drape you with cloth or paper drapes to cover all areas except for the vagina.

Crowning Of The Baby's Head

The last contraction before the delivery of the baby's head may cause an unpleasant sensation—as if you were splitting open. Actually, the baby is causing the ligaments around the coccyx (base of the spinal column) to stretch. During a contraction, the doctor may give the local anesthesia for the *episiotomy,* an incision to enlarge the vaginal opening and to prevent the tearing of the *perineum,* the area between the vagina and rectum. However, if the episiotomy is made during a contraction, it will be painless—the pressure of the baby's head on the thin tissue of the perineum creates a natural anesthesia.

With the next few contractions, the outline of the baby's head can be seen stretching through the perineum, and it looks like a large grapefruit. This is referred to as the crowning of the baby's head, and it is a very exciting moment. Usually, your baby's head will be born with just a few more pushes.

Most babies make their appearance headfirst, face toward the floor. This *vertex* position means that the baby is leaving the uterus head down. The back of the baby's head (occiput) is toward the mother's coccyx when labor begins; as the baby descends into the pelvis, the head turns so the soft cartilage of the nose will be against the mother's tailbone (coccyx). This is the most efficient way for a baby to slip past the pubic bone and into the birth canal. As the doctor gently guides the baby's head out, the head spontaneously turns to the left or right to line up with the baby's as-yet-unborn shoulders. The doctor will next locate the cord. Should it be around the baby's neck, he would try to draw the cord down around the occiput to prevent compression by the shoulder, and when possible, clamp and cut the cord—painless to mother and baby.

With the next contraction the upper or anterior shoulder will be delivered, and the rest of the baby will slither out, completing the second stage. When the umbilical cord stops pulsating, it is clamped and cut. Your baby is now a separate individual!

Some babies may take their first breath and begin to cry, suddenly turning red even before they are completely born. But often the baby will not begin to cry until the attendant has removed the mucus from his nose and mouth. This is nothing to be alarmed about. In either case the sound of your baby's first cry is something you will never forget.

If for some reason you are unable to expel the baby on your own, your child will be delivered by forceps. The forceps resemble a pair of salad tongs with long, curved blades to fit the shape of the baby's head. Each blade is inserted into the vagina separately and placed carefully on either side of the baby's head. The two handles cross and lock together, and the baby's head is slowly and gently extracted. The delivery of the rest of the baby is the same as in a spontaneous delivery. The primary indication for a forceps delivery is fetal distress, indicated by a slowed heart rate. Other indications are excessive pressure on the baby's head resulting from a short, stormy labor or an extremely long one; incorrect position of the baby's head; and inability of the mother to push the baby out due to use of conduction anesthesia or exhaustion.

Birth

After the head emerges, it turns as the shoulders rotate. The head is gently and firmly supported by the doctor. As contractions continue, the head is guided upward over the receding and thickening perineum, and the rest of the body slides out. The baby is born.

Baby's Appearance At Birth

If your baby has begun to breathe before he is completely born, he may have a normal flush. Otherwise the baby will be a bluish color at first, or in the case of a black baby, gray to black in color. The doctor will suction any blood or mucus from the baby's nose and mouth. (The stereotype of the physician holding the newborn by its heels and giving it a slap on the backside is outdated. Slapping on the back is only done in extreme cases, since it can cause trauma to the baby.) Resuscitation equipment stands by in case it is needed. If the baby has difficulty in breathing, immediate assistance is necessary as there may otherwise be damage to the brain cells due to lack of oxygen.

The baby will be wet-looking and may be covered with a white, creamy substance called *vernix,* which has been protecting his skin in utero and has acted as a greasing agent as the baby moved along the vaginal canal. (Some babies will also be spotted with blood from the birth canal.) Another newborn characteristic observed in some babies is the appearance of a fine downy covering called *lanugo,* which disappears within a few days.

You may be surprised by the odd, elongated shape of the baby's head. The baby's skull is not completely hard as it comes down the birth canal, and it molds to adapt to the shape of the vagina. The occiput, which has been acting as a battering ram, may be swollen (caput), but the head will reshape to a more rounded appearance within several days. If forceps were used, the baby may have forceps marks, which will also disappear in a few days.

At one minute, and again at five minutes after birth, your baby's condition will be evaluated visually by what is known as the *Apgar Score*. This system, developed by Dr. Virginia Apgar, uses the vital signs of heart rate, respiratory rate, muscle tone, cry, and color to determine the newborn's status. Two points are given for each of the five categories. The one-minute score may indicate that the baby requires assistance. The five-minute score is the important one in relation to how a baby will fare later in life. A maximum of ten may be obtained. This procedure simply allows the attendant to quickly assess your newborn's health; it is not a "test."

The nurse will also place a drop of silver-nitrate or antibiotic solution in each of your baby's eyes, which is then rinsed out with water. This eliminates the chance of infection or blindness from undetected gonorrhea in the mother, a procedure required by law. The baby is then given a nameband with your name, sex of the baby, date and time of birth, and a duplicate is given to the mother to prevent any mixup. He is then wrapped in a blanket and placed in a warming bed to help maintain his body temperature. If your husband is present, the nurse will hand the baby to him for a moment.

An exception to this procedure is the so-called "modified" Leboyer delivery. Developed by a French obstetrician, it calls for a quiet, dimly lit delivery room. Immediately after birth the baby is placed on the mother's stomach and gently massaged. The umbilical cord is not cut until it stops pulsating. (The warm water bath advocated by Leboyer is sometimes omitted in this country.) The aim of all this is to make the birth more pleasant for the baby who, it is claimed, faces the trauma of bright lights and noise after a peaceful existence in the womb. More and more hospitals are now allowing this type of procedure to complement Lamaze deliveries.

Delivery Of The Placenta

The delivery of the afterbirth or placenta marks the *third and final stage* of the birth process. During pregnancy the placenta is attached to the wall of the uterus and connected to the baby via the umbilical cord. It provides the vehicle through which nutrients and oxygen from the mother pass to the baby and wastes are removed. After the child's birth, the uterus becomes much smaller and stops contracting to "rest" after the strenuous work of delivery. In a few minutes it begins to contract again. This time the purpose is to free the placenta from the wall of the uterus, then to squeeze the placenta down into the vagina where it is removed by the obstetrician.

As soon as the placenta is delivered, the doctor examines it carefully to be sure it is complete. This organ is composed of 20 or so placentae, sort of like a honeycomb of smooth tile-like pieces. If part of the placenta remains in the uterus, the hormone released by the placenta will stimulate excessive bleeding. Most doctors perform a manual removal of the placenta if it has not been expelled several minutes after the baby. The placenta is red and "meaty," and its appearance may be a bit shocking to the uninitiated.

Excessive bleeding is usually not a problem after delivery. The blood loss at delivery averages eight ounces. Since the blood plasma volume increases about a quart during pregnancy, the loss of half a pint is easily tolerated. Nature has arranged the muscles of the uterus so that they can "close off" the blood vessels in the lining to prevent excessive bleeding. But it is essential that the uterus remain fairly firm after delivery in order for it to function properly. The doctor may firmly knead the uterus through the abdominal wall or use hormones such as Oxytocin or Ergonovine to make it contract.

With the birth completed, the doctor repairs the episiotomy using catgut sutures. The stitches will be absorbed in 15 to 20 days and need not be removed. Some authorities recommend that an ice pack be placed on the episiotomy site immediately after repair to help decrease the tissue swelling and ease the discomfort that is a common postpartum complaint.

The doctor will check your baby carefully, and then the baby will be brought back to you. This is the moment you have been looking forward to for many months, and it will surely be an exciting one. If your husband has participated in the birth, the three of you will have a chance to get acquainted now. Some mothers even nurse their baby for the first time right on the delivery table (ask ahead if this is permitted).

Unfortunately, in many hospitals mother and baby are soon separated. Baby will be taken to the nursery to be weighed, bathed and diapered. You will remain in the recovery room for several hours so the staff can monitor your blood pressure and bleeding from the placental site.

Now that the delivery is over, you may feel euphoric—a bit "high" at the thought of what you've just accomplished. Some women, however, feel a bit "empty" and depressed as they wait for their babies to be brought to them (your baby may remain in the nursery for six to 24 hours).

However, many parents are now requesting private time alone with their newborn immediately after delivery. During this time, called *bonding,* parents wel-

Expulsion of Placenta

Placenta almost separated and membranes loosened. They are then expelled.

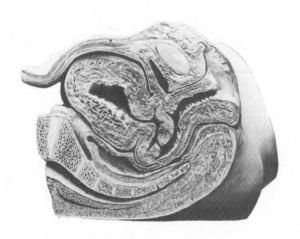

The uterus, after exit of the placenta, sags into the pelvis.

come their newborn into the world through skin-to-skin contact, cuddling, and talking to the baby.

In addition to bonding, many hospitals now offer rooming-in or family-centered maternity plans that allow mother and newborn more time together. Check the hospital policy to see if you can keep the baby with you at all times or if there is a modified plan where you can have your baby taken back to the nursery if you need rest.

Your hospital stay may be anywhere from two days to a week or more (average is three days), depending on the type of delivery you had and, of course, your rate of recovery. Cesarean patients are generally hospitalized for a full week, but by the fourth day they may feel as strong as women who have had an uncomplicated birth. If there were no complications, you should be allowed out of bed the day of delivery. (Early ambulation can lead to a quicker recovery and decreased bowel and bladder problems.)

It is, however, a good idea to take it easy even if you think you feel terrific. One way to do this is to pace the number of visitors you have in the hospital (and again when you get home, where you may be expected to play hostess and feed and entertain your guests). Your husband can tactfully suggest to friends and relatives that you will be delighted to have them come and see the new baby— just as soon as you feel up to it.

The Immediate Postpartum Period

Within a few hours of delivery, you will have already lost about 12 pounds. Your tummy will not flatten out for about a week although your uterus will have begun to shrink back to its pre-pregnant size. The entire process takes about six weeks, and this period is known as the *puerperium* (from the Latin for ''having brought forth a child''). When the puerperium begins, the uterus is a two-pound mass of muscle; by the end of six weeks it has shrunk to three ounces. This is referred to as *involution* of the uterus.

Contractions continue after delivery so that the uterus may involute normally, and they may cause discomfort similar to menstrual cramps (known as ''after-pains''). After-pains may last for several days and may be especially noticeable during nursing sessions. This is because involution is stimulated by nursing; thus the uterus of a nursing mother shrinks more rapidly. After-pains can usually be relieved by simple analgesics such as aspirin.

The *lochia* is the postpartum uterine discharge. Immediately following delivery the lochia is bright red, and the amount is noted by the nurse. As the uterus shrinks back to its normal size (probably slightly larger than before pregnancy), the lochia will become brown and cease altogether. (It may, however, become red again during the first days at home if you overdo your normal activities. Reduce your activity, and if the bleeding is progressive, call your doctor.) The length of bleeding varies considerably from woman to woman, but the average is about 21 days. There is also no set rule for the reappearance of menstruation after delivery. (Sometimes menstruation is confused with a heavy lochia about one month after delivery.) If you are nursing, you may not resume menstruating until the baby is weaned although you could begin to ovulate (and accidentally become pregnant) without resuming menstruation.

Increased urination is common between the second and fifth days after delivery. In this way the body rids itself of the extra tissue water (two to three quarts) that has accumulated during pregnancy. Rarely, a woman may be unable to urinate after a long and difficult labor or a forceps delivery and may have to be catheterized for a day or two. There is also a tendency to become constipated during the puerperium, and hemorrhoids may occur as a result of pushing during delivery. As long as you don't strain, you won't tear your stitches. A diet with sufficient fluids will keep the bowel movements soft. Early ambulation and elimination of bedpan use make constipation far less of a problem than it used to be. Warm baths and soothing ointments can help relieve discomfort from hemorrhoids.

The episiotomy stitches may itch or be painful, and this area may continue to be tender for several weeks. Among the remedies for a painful episiotomy site are: 1) sitz bath—warm, shallow soaking of episiotomy; 2) witch hazel compress, and 3) medicated ointments or sprays. To help ease the strain when you sit, tighten your buttocks as if you were holding a dime between them.

The breasts will begin to secrete *colostrum* (a sticky, yellow fluid) after delivery. If you are nursing, the colostrum will provide the baby with its major source of nourishment the first few days after delivery. Your baby may not seem interested in nursing at first—he is tired. Don't worry—patience and persistence will pay off. On the third day his interest in eating will increase.

When your milk comes in, on the third day after delivery, your breasts may become suddenly larger, firm, hot, and painful. This is called *engorgement,* and it rarely lasts more than 24 to 36 hours. You can avoid it by applying ice packs between feedings. Breast-feeding on demand also helps relieve this situation. Women who are not going to breast-feed may be given medication to prevent engorgement of the breasts. Regardless of whether you are going to breast-feed, you should wear a good bra 24 hours a day for two weeks, starting right away, to help prevent engorgement of the breasts.

The *"baby blues"* (or postpartum depression) are a common phenomena among new mothers. Doctors put part of the blame on fatigue and hormone changes, but you may also feel depressed because your tummy hasn't immediately become as flat as you'd hoped it would; because you didn't feel a rush of maternal feelings at the first sight of your baby (this will come in time); or because you feel awkward in caring for your baby.

Usually these blues last only a few days and are accompanied by the *milk letdown reflex*. Some women never feel depressed while others feel blue for several months after the baby is born. Usually, as you become more confident in your mothering abilities and adjust to your new lifestyle, your emotions will improve. It will also help if you set aside some time for yourself—to read, take a walk—and for occasional outings with your husband (time to spend as a couple, not as parents). If, however, feelings of depression persist, you may need the help of a professional counselor.

Going home with your new baby will be an exciting (and perhaps a bit scary) moment. You may feel overwhelmed by your responsibility for this new life. Try to relax and remember that most new parents have a few doubts. Ideally, you should have someone to help with the housework for the first week or so—a friend, relative, or paid help. You'll need plenty of rest. Don't overexert yourself.

If you have any unusual symptoms—especially increased vaginal bleeding—call your doctor at once. And don't be tempted to skip the six weeks' checkup just because you are feeling fine. It's important that your doctor examine you to be certain that your recovery is normal.

The first few days and weeks at home with your new baby will be a real time of adjustment. Many parents say they had no idea how much time and trouble it took to care for a baby. They also say they wouldn't have missed having one for anything!

Quick Dictionary Of Terms

Apgar score—Rates newborn's health on a scale of 1-10 after visual examination performed at one and again at five minutes after birth

colostrum—thin, yellow fluid secreted by the breasts before the milk comes in. Thought to contain antibodies

crowning—when the top of the baby's head becomes visible at the vaginal opening just before birth

episiotomy—incision in the perineum to prevent it from tearing

fontanels—soft spots on the baby's head. There are two: anterior (front of the skull) and posterior (back of the skull)

forceps—special surgical applicators sometimes used to deliver a baby

in utero—in the womb

involution—process by which the uterus returns (shrinks) to normal size

lanugo—fine downy hair that may appear on the newborn but disappears within a few days

lithotomy position—most common delivery position in this country. Woman is lying on her back with legs up and held apart in stirrups

lochia—postpartum uterine discharge

perineum—muscular area between the vagina and rectum

postpartum depression—(also called ''baby blues'')—a short period of depression that often follows childbirth. Thought to be related to hormone changes

vernix (also vernix caseosa)—a white creamy substance that covers the newborn skin

Before Birth: How Does Your Baby Grow?

by Donna Buys, R.N.

One of the most fascinating subjects in any field of study is how the fetus grows—from a tiny speck of tissue weighing next to nothing into a seven-pound living human being.

The fetus as it looks at 39 days

These drawings show the development of the fetus from the 3rd month to the 9th month. During the first two months, the embryo has grown to a fetus, measuring about 1-1/8 inches long and weighing about 1/30 of an ounce. Face and features have started to form, and the limbs begin to show distinct divisions into arms, hands, knees, lower legs, and feet.

The stage is set when the ovum or egg is discharged from the ovary and begins a 10-day journey through the fallopian tube leading to the uterus. Conception occurs about one-third of the way through the fallopian tube when a sperm (one of millions in one act of ejaculation) plunges into the ovum. Together they continue on to the uterus.

The sex of the baby is determined during its first day of life by the genetic makeup of the sperm. The union of the sperm and ovum is an electrifying experience which initiates a vigorous growth of cells through dividing and subdividing. At the end of two days, the *zygote*, a tiny speck of tissue, grows to a ball of 16 cells called the *morula*, which resembles a mulberry.

By the third day of life, the "mulberry" mass has reached the uterus, and by the end of the first week, it has embedded itself into the wall of the uterus. Meanwhile, an inner and outer layer becomes apparent. The inner layer will develop into an *embryo.* The outer layer is the feeding layer. This feeding layer burrows into the uterus and makes contact with the mother's bloodstream.

Soon after the inner layer is receiving nourishment, it changes rapidly into the *ectoderm* (an outer covering layer), the *mesoderm* (a middle layer), and the *entoderm* (an internal layer).

The baby's distinguishing characteristics develop from these layers. From the ectoderm come the skin, hair, nails, sweat glands, mucus membranes of the nose, mouth and throat, enamel of the teeth, and the nervous system. From the *mesoderm* come the muscles, bones, cartilage, dentin of the teeth, ligaments, breast tissue, kidneys, ureters, ovaries, testes, heart, blood, blood vessels, and linings of the heart and abdominal cavity. From the *entoderm* come the linings of the digestive tract, the respiratory tract, and the bladder.

Before any of these characteristics develop, the bag of waters or *amniotic fluid* develops around the embryo. This fluid provides protection. It keeps the fetus at an even temperature, cushions it against possible injury, and provides a medium in which it can easily move.

When physicians estimate the expected date of delivery, they assume that conception took place two weeks after the first day of the last menstrual period. Based on the 28-day menstrual cycle, they calculate the length of pregnancy in

Third Month

Your baby is now about 3 inches long and weighs about 1 ounce. The hands are fully formed with fingers and nails all present.

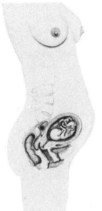

Fourth Month

Your baby is now about 7 inches long and weighs about 4 ounces. The head is disproportionately large; bones are distinct.

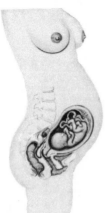

Fifth Month

About 10 inches long and about 1/2-1 pound, the internal organs are maturing rapidly. Eyelids are fused, and some hair appears.

Sixth Month

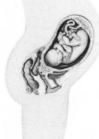

Your baby is now 12-14 inches long and weighs 1-1/2 pounds. Fingernails extend to the ends of fingers; eyelashes are formed.

Seventh Month

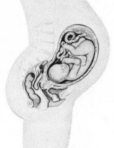

The baby's weight has almost doubled since last month and it is about 3 inches longer. It is still red and wrinkled.

Eighth Month

By the end of this month, the baby will add 2-1/2 more pounds and lengthen to almost 18 inches. The head bones are soft.

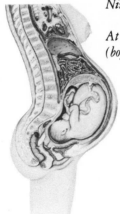

Ninth Month

At full term the baby weighs about 7 pounds (girl) or 7-1/2 (boy) and is about 20 inches long.

lunar months of 28 days' duration. Therefore, there are actually 9 1/2 lunar months to a normal pregnancy.

The *First Month* "birthday" takes place two weeks after the first missed period. At this time the embryo is about a quarter of an inch long, including the "tail" that it has at this stage. The backbone is apparent but is so bent that the head almost touches the tip of the tail. The head is very prominent, representing almost one-third of the entire embryo. The eyes, ears, and nose are apparent. The tube which will form the heart makes a rounded bulge on the body wall and is already pulsating regularly and propelling blood through microscopic arteries. The digestive tract is a long, slender tube leading from the mouth to an expansion that will become the stomach, connected with the beginnings of the intestines. Arms and legs are small bumps that resemble buds.

The embryo has grown to a fetus by the end of the *Second Month*. It measures about one inch from head to buttocks, and its weight is about one-thirtieth of an ounce. The brain develops during this month, and the face becomes unmistakably human. The external genitalia become apparent, but it is difficult to distinguish between male and female. Arms, legs, fingers, toes, elbows, thighs, feet, and knees are apparent at this stage. The umbilical cord is formed by this time, and the long bones and internal organs are developing.

At the end of the *Third Month,* the fetus measures a little more than three inches and weighs almost an ounce. The sex still cannot be distinguished. Baby teeth, bones, fingernails and toenails have begun to develop. Kidneys have developed and are secreting small amounts of urine into the bladder, which later escape into the amniotic fluid. The fetus may move at this time, but movements are too weak to be felt by the mother. By this time the *placenta* has formed. It nourishes the fetus through the umbilical cord, which is cut after the birth of the baby.

During the first four months, the fetus has quadrupled its weight every month. So, at the end of the *Fourth Month*, it is six and a half inches long from head to toe and is four ounces in weight. The sex of the baby is very obvious. The bag of waters is enlarged to the size of an orange.

The fetus is ten inches long and weighs about eight ounces by the end of the *Fifth Month*. It is covered by a fine downy hair called *lanugo*. About this time the mother can expect to feel slight fluttering movements in her abdomen, and the physician will be able to hear the fetal heartbeat.

At the end of the *Sixth Month*, the fetus is twelve inches long and weighs one and a half pounds. It looks like a miniature baby except that its skin is very wrinkled and red and there is almost no fat between its skin and bones. The skin begins to develop a protective cheesy coating called *vernix caseosa*. This fatty substance may be an eighth of an inch thick when the baby is born.

By the end of the *Seventh Month,* the fetus is about fifteen inches long and weighs about two and a half pounds. If born prematurely at this time, the fetus would have a one-in-ten chance of surviving. This chance increases with the age of the fetus.

The fetus grows an inch and a half and gains one and a half pounds so that at the end of the *Eighth Month* it is about sixteen to eighteen inches long and weighs about four pounds. It looks much like an old man with its wrinkled skin covered with the lanugo and vernix caseosa. If the fetus is born at this time, the chances are as high as two out of three that it would live with the help of an incubator and good nursing care.

The fetus is practically a mature infant at the end of the *Ninth Lunar Month*. It measures about nineteen inches and weighs around six pounds. Fat has now accumulated beneath the skin so that the body has become more round and the skin less wrinkled and red. During the last two months, the fetus has gained an average of one-half pound a week.

At the middle of the tenth lunar month, full term has been reached. The fetus is twenty inches long and weighs about seven pounds if it's a girl, and seven and a half pounds if it's a boy. The fine, downy hair has just about disappeared. The fingernails are hard and long enough so that they are sometimes cut shortly after birth to prevent the infant from scratching himself. The lungs are fully developed at this time and begin to function with the infant's first cry.

Thus, from a zygote to an embryo to a fetus, an infant develops and is born.

A Guide To Cesarean Delivery
by Pat Jackowitz, R.N.

"When my childbirth instructor gave a lecture that began, 'Twenty percent of all women who give birth will have their babies by Cesarean section,' I barely listened. This could not apply to me since I had had a 'perfect' pregnancy, and I had practiced my Lamaze exercises faithfully with my husband as coach. It would be the woman next to me that would have the section, not me. The instructor encouraged us to go home and think about what impact a Cesarean birth would have on the three of us, both emotionally and physically."

Thus began many birth reports received after delivery. Today Cesarean births have increased in this country by ten percent. This is basically a result of the introduction of fetal monitoring and the changes in management of breech deliveries.

The term Cesarean section refers to the surgical operation by an abdominal incision to remove the baby from the uterus. The decision to deliver by a Cesarean varies, but the five most common reasons are: failure to progress, cephalo-pelvic disproportion (CPD), malpresentation (breech birth), fetal distress, and bleeding. Other reasons include multiple births, diabetes, placenta previa, placenta abruptio, and eclampsia.

Fetal Monitoring

Fetal monitoring gives a continual picture of what is going on inside the uterus. It is an aid to doctors in detecting oxygen problems, and it is an asset to the parents to be able to watch contractions begin before the body feels them.

The monitor, a mechanical device that has two discs which are placed on the abdomen between the navel and the pubic hairline and held in place by a belt, gives dual information. It can indicate the baby's heart rate and measure the strength and duration of a contraction. With this information the physician can determine the progress of labor and assist the parents in working with each contraction.

Cephalo-Pelvic Disproportion—CPD

The size of a baby's head varies as does the mother's pelvis. The pelvic canal is irregular in shape, and a full-term baby will often not pass through the pelvis. Prior to the onset of labor, the baby's head should descend into the pelvis below the pubic inlet. But many women begin labor with a "floating" head. The baby has not descended, and the doctor must see how the labor progresses. If during labor the head does not descend, the physician will then send the mother for pelvic x-rays to determine the size of the baby in relation to the mother's pelvis. If the baby's head is too large or if the mother's pelvis is unusually shaped, a Cesarean section is indicated.

Failure To Progress

During pregnancy the top of the uterus grows to support the pregnancy. During labor the lower third of the uterus, the cervix, must change to allow for delivery. The cervix is long and as thick as a bottleneck before the onset of labor. Contractions cause the cervix to efface (thin down) and dilate, and to be ready for delivery the cervix must be 100 percent effaced and 10 centimeters dilated.

Often during labor a woman will have contractions but the cervix does not dilate. It will remain partially open without making any progress. The physician cannot let a woman labor indefinitely and may decide to give her a "trial labor" stimulated by medication. Through the use of Oxytocin (a synthetic hormone of the pituitary gland), the doctor can increase the intensity and frequency of contractions, hoping to cause the cervix to dilate. If the cervix fails to dilate, the physician must do a Cesarean.

Malpresentation

The most common malpresentation of birth is a breech delivery. Instead of the baby's head being the presenting part, it is the feet or buttocks of the baby. For a woman having her first baby, it is almost certain that a breech will be delivered by Cesarean section. Since the pelvis is untried, the obstetrician does not know whether a head will pass through the pelvis once the rest of the baby is delivered, and he does not want to prolong the delivery stage. In such a case, when the baby's head is delivered, the umbilical cord could be caught between the baby's head and the pelvis, decreasing oxygen to the baby. Some obstetricians feel that a Cesarean delivery is indicated in this situation, but opinions vary as to whether or not it is necessary. Some physicians will try to externally rotate the breech position, although this isn't always successful and runs the risk of separating the placenta prematurely.

Another form of malpresentation is a transverse position. The baby is lying across the mother's pelvis. Depending upon circumstances, the obstetrician may try to rotate the position of the baby. But this is not always successful. When it is, a woman may then have a vaginal delivery.

Fetal Distress

If at any time during labor the fetal heart rate slows momentarily and does not return to a normal heartbeat, a woman in labor would be turned on her left side and given oxygen to breathe. If the heartbeat does not increase to an acceptable level (120 to 160) with this procedure, this is an indication for an emergency Cesarean section. If monitoring machines were not being used to check the heart rate, the nurse would listen to the baby's heartbeat with a fetascope.

Bleeding

Bleeding during pregnancy can be both a problem and an annoyance. There are times when bleeding occurs and the physician does not know why, so he watches more carefully during pregnancy. In labor, however, progressive red bleeding and / or one continual contraction are danger signs. If this were to occur while a woman was at home, she should call her doctor immediately and proceed to the hospital.

The Operation

It is possible to be awake during the Cesarean and to be aware of what is happening to you. Regional anesthesia (epidural, caudal, or spinal) will numb you from below the breasts down to the toes. You will not feel pain with the surgery, but *you will feel pressure if touched.* It takes twenty minutes for the anesthesia to be fully effective.

Regional anesthesia cannot be used if there is fetal distress or bleeding since it can cause a drop in an already troubled blood pressure. In such instances, general anesthesia is indicated. If you require general anesthesia, you will receive a drug intravenously to put you to sleep, or a mask will be placed over your nose and mouth, and you will be asked to take several deep breaths. All the necessary preliminaries for a Cesarean are completed prior to the administration of anesthesia. This reduces the total anesthesia received by the baby.

Such procedures include the administration of medication to dry up secretion in the mouth, a complete pubic shave, possibly the insertion of a catheter to drain urine from the bladder until the surgery is completed (or a day or so later), and the beginning of an intravenous drip to introduce the medication during surgery.

The atmosphere is very relaxed. The surgery will take about one hour, ten minutes to get the baby out and fifty minutes more to close the incision. The physician will tell you that you're going to feel a tug and then you *may* or *may not* hear a cry. The baby is born, the doctor tells you the sex, and all the while he is suctioning out amniotic fluid from the baby's nose and mouth. A child born by section is much wetter and has more fluid than one born vaginally. The following 48 hours the baby will be observed closely.

After you have seen the baby, the obstetrician may request that you be put to sleep in order to relax the muscles and help close the incision. When you awake in the recovery room, you will have a bandage on your abdomen, and you may have a sore throat. You will stay in the recovery room until your blood pressure is stabilized, the uterus is firm, and the anesthesia has worn off. It could be several hours. As the anesthesia wears off, you will feel pain since you have had major surgery. Medication for the pain is available to you. Do not hesitate to take it the first day or so.

For the first 24 hours following your Cesarean, you will receive all nourishment intravenously. Subsequently, light fluids and food will be introduced. On the second or third day, the bandage is removed, and you will see the incision for the first time. It could extend from your belly button to your pubic hairline, or it could be a "bikini" cut, which is in a smile shape above the pubic hairline.

Most women are aware of gas pains the first few days, which can be alleviated by moving about and defecating. If you are planning to breast-feed your baby, the first time or two you may find it awkward, but do persist. Remember that the incision heals and the intravenous equipment is removed in time. You will probably be in the hospital about a week.

Current Trends

Parents who have experienced Cesarean births are now organizing groups for the purpose of helping other parents understand the operation and alternatives for the future. Many hospitals are now allowing fathers in the delivery room for some Cesareans. Men who have worked to coach their wives during labor and participate in the birth of their child find that when a section is indicated, the coach is separated from his wife, wondering whether mother and baby are all right. The mother has a sense of being abandoned. To overcome the sense of abandonment, fathers are now being allowed in the delivery room if a mother is having regional anesthesia. He is not there to observe the surgery but can sit next to the mother and exchange conversation and offer support. Parents who have experienced this form of birth feel that they have not been deprived of the participation that is so rightfully theirs.

The Bonding Experience
by Tunie Munson

How to share the first hours with your newborn.

For partners committed to sharing the joys and responsibilities of parenting from the start, who want professional services and the expertise of a hospital staff, and who want an extended and private time together to welcome their baby—the bonding experience is irresistible and important.

Bonding means forming a strong attachment with your child. Though most parents eventually bond with their children, the chance to do so immediately, while still in the hospital, is one which more and more parents are now demanding.

Neonatologists Marshall Klaus and John Kennell, in their book *Maternal-Infant Bonding,* indicate the benefits to the infant of such early and extended interaction: fewer infections, better weight gain, less crying, more smiles and laughter, greater subsequent language development and possible higher intelligence, and increased chance for survival—especially in the case of premature babies. Research has also pointed to potential pluses for parents, including less incidence of child abuse and other parenting disorders, more protective behavior, increased self-confidence about parenting abilities, faster postpartum recuperation, and extended weeks of breast-feeding. So bonding may have profound implications for how parents parent.

Intent on repeating results, scientists will continue to study the phenomenon before they insist on bonding as a requisite for every birth experience. But parents don't have the scientist's opportunity to wait and see. If you are going to have a baby, perhaps you are convinced that sharing memorable first hours as a family is reason enough to try bonding. Unfortunately, simply wanting to bond does not guarantee that you'll be able to, as many disappointed, disgruntled parents have learned.

One couple admits they knew little about the specifics of bonding when they asked their doctor to include it in their childbirth experience.

''We assumed he knew all about it, that he would tell us what to do,'' the woman reports. ''Well, he didn't.''

Her husband adds, "Donna had the baby on her chest for a few minutes in the delivery room. That was it. Later we discovered that bonding entails a lot more."

Another couple had researched ahead of time. Their doctor had agreed to go along with their wishes.

"He really encouraged us," says Susan. "But he wasn't on duty in rhe middle of the night when I delivered. The attending physician, an associate, didn't know about our arrangements. The nurses were suspicious. They told us we'd have to wait for our doctor's approval and whisked the baby away."

One woman (who took the necessary steps to ensure bonding) confesses that subtle intimidation prompted her to refrain from skin-to-skin contact with her newborn, a feature of the bonding process.

"They had no heat panel so the nurses insisted on taking my baby's temperature every few minutes. They warned me that if his temperature changed, they'd have to move my baby to the nursery for observation. I was so worried that I didn't dare remove his blanket. As it turned out, he got too warm being all wrapped up.

Starting Your Own Campaign

If you are a prospective parent who has access to a hospital that encourages family-centered care that includes bonding, you can sit back and celebrate. However, many couples live too far from such hospitals or homelike delivery centers, and they need to recognize that initially only *their* efforts will determine whether they can bond with their baby.

Mustering the initiative and energy to mount a campaign is not easy. We, like others, had reservations to overcome first. Could my husband avoid job conflicts during his mini-paternity leave in the days after birth? Would the new father feel like a third wheel in the hospital setting? Would I be able to room in with my baby and still get the rest I needed? Could we adequately care for our hours-old baby alone?

Another look at existing information on bonding convinced us of its merits. And we also learned that resistance from medical personnel can stem from staff-centered rather than patient-centered policies or a refusal to give up traditional authority. In a feature on bonding in *The Journal of Pediatrics (July 1977)*, Dr. Betty Lozoff (along with other colleagues) noted: "There is no medical reason why healthy mothers and babies should not be together from the time of birth to the time of discharge from the hospital."

Though we were warned that the hospital rules were ironclad and there was no hope for change, we had already begun a campaign to win hospital approval of the bonding experiment. Because we at last convinced the staff to let us try the innovations, hospital policy did not, in the end, deny us the happiness of intimately welcoming our baby into the world.

In the first hour after birth, when the alert and quiet baby is ideally suited for the initial meeting with the parents, we marveled at our daughter's ability to study us, to meet our gazes and respond to our touch. The cuddling and talking seemed to have a calming effect on her. (Research now indicates that having one primary caretaker in the first ten days, rather than multiple caretakers as in nursery care, has a stabilizing effect on infants.) Nurses remarked about the contrast between our daughter's serene and contented demeanor while in the room with us, and her crying during a brief stint in the nursery.

By the time we headed home, both of us had already held, bathed, soothed, cuddled, diapered, and dressed our baby daily. We had been together when one or the other of us needed to express worries about minor birth complications (which seemed overwhelming at the time) or to relive the event of birth. What's more, as new parents, we felt a surprising self-confidence about our parenting abilities. Even the pediatric nurses expressed amazement that we rarely called our pediatrician (unlike other parents) in the weeks that followed birth.

How To Do It Your *Way*

Our persistence paid off. We won the right to bond and the rewards inherent in the experience. And it is within the powers of every committed couple to do the same. The following steps will help ensure that the outcome of your effort is as rewarding.

First, read about bonding, months before the due date, if possible. The best inspirational source is *Maternal-Infant Bonding* by Marshall Klaus and John Kennell (available in paperback from the C.V. Mosby Co., 1976). It offers convincing arguments for including bonding in every birth experience. It details procedures to follow, reports findings of bonding effects on both parent and infant behavior, and includes chapters on bonding with premature infants and newborns with malformations. Also helpful is Elliott H. McCleary's *New Miracles of Childbirth,* particularly the last chapter on "Childbirth—Family Style."

Excerpts from such sources go a long way toward convincing medical personnel that your actions are motivated by enlightenment and not whim. Providing the doctor and hospital staffer with copies of relevant passages for easy reference simplifies the communication between you.

In addition to citing specific data on bonding, we collected quotes from respected experts like author and doctor H.M.I. Liley, who noted in *Modern Motherhood*:

"When he has been medically checked and found to be sound in the delivery room, the very kindest thing that can be done for the battered, weary little newborn is to give him a warm cuddling and reassurance as quickly as possible... It is artificial and unnecessary to 'protect' the newborn from bacteria (unless he is premature) by isolating him in an antiseptic nursery, away from his mother's arms and emotions. The newborn must get harmless bacteria all over his skin surface as soon as possible if he is to survive this germ-filled world. He also needs to be exposed to his first pleasurable emotion. Ideally his exposure to an entirely new world should come from his mother."

Expending energy on collecting quotes may be unnecessary, of course, if you find a supportive and enlightened doctor or hospital staff (and see to it that one recommends the other). And by making your first visit to the doctor as a couple, you show your solidarity and mutual commitment to the bonding experience.

Some prospective parents, aware of a local hospital that endorses bonding, contact the hospital administrator first and ask for referral to a practitioner who has already encouraged family-centered care. The International Childbirth Education Association (Box 20852, Milwaukee, Wisconsin 53220) can provide information regarding which, if any, hospitals in your area include such care in their programs. Another helpful source is the American College of Nurse Midwives (1000 Vermont Avenue, N.W., Washington, D.C. 20005).

An Outline Of Requests

By communicating in advance with hospital personnel (an administrator first and later heads of the obstetrical and neonatal staffs), we spared ourselves the agony of on-the-spot conflicts. For instance, we discovered resistance to our presence as a family in the large recovery area (where other new mothers were routinely separated from their newborns in another observation nursery). The staff also refused to promise us a labor room for private recovery together. They insisted that bonding immediately after birth would, therefore, not be feasible. We had weeks to counter via letter that a hospital corridor would suffice, that extended time together following delivery was crucial. Days before the due date, they finally conceded.

Doctor- and staff-approved orders can be waiting for pickup upon your arrival at the hospital. All nurses noted our clipboard data at a staff meeting weeks before delivery since our requests were so numerous.

Do not underestimate the energy-saving value of written instructions to substitute for spontaneous debates at a time when your concentration is divided. Be sure that, ultimately, these details end up on that clipboard:

1. Ensure that medical personnel delay the routine application of silver nitrate to the newborn's eyes until after the first encounter with the parents in the hour after delivery. The awake baby can then respond to your gazes and physical cues.

2. Ensure privacy for your family after birth. An empty labor room or partitioned recovery area is ideal. This arrangement especially encourages important skin-to-skin contact of the naked infant on the mother's bare chest. It promotes fondling and touching of the infant by both parents. Some hospitals provide an overhead radiant heat panel to maintain the baby's body temperature. However, a proven safe alternative is to loosely cover mother and thoroughly dried baby with a warm blanket.

3. Receive instruction after childbirth on how to suction mucus from the newborn (a relatively simple procedure using a rubber syringe) should the need arise. Determine how to summon immediate aid.

4. Abolish the father's visitor status. He should have access to mother and infant all day in order to give support and to bond with his infant.

5. Request a rooming-in plan that guarantees presence of the baby a minimum of five hours a day. Some mothers ask to have the baby day and night. Others appreciate the flexibility of having the baby brought during the night according to the infant's needs (demand feeding) and not according to the hospital feeding schedule.

6. A notation to include siblings in the experience is important. They should have a chance—as soon after delivery as possible—to meet the newborn, and if parents and children desire, to continue daily reunions until homecoming time.

More and more hospitals are honoring the demands of enlightened and committed parents, and they are becoming partners with parents in humanizing and personalizing this important event.

After the struggle of childbirth, the moments of relief and triumph signaled beginnings for us. In privacy together our family moved beyond the miracle to introductions. We had a space of time without the distractions of the world. Those first hours beyond birth can be a time for touching, reminiscing, bonding—a time to love.

To Expectant Fathers:
What To Do If She Panics During Labor

by Sally Langendoen, R.N.

A childbirth instructor tells how to help your wife if she panics during labor.

You faithfully attended the preparation for childbirth classes together with your wife. You practiced the breathing techniques with her every night. You drove her to the hospital in good time. And for the past several hours, you have been reminding her to relax and begin timing her contractions. But what if, in spite of your hard work and soothing ministrations, she panics? Suddenly a contraction overwhelms her. What would you do?

A few years ago it happened to me. My labor began in a straightforward fashion. I was very much in control of the contractions until, suddenly, they started to come very fast and very hard. Wave after wave seemed to crash over me. I had trouble catching my breath. I wasn't sure I could go on. My husband felt quite helpless, too, because he didn't know what to do or what to tell me.

Then my obstetrician walked into the room. "Get me some Demerol," I cried out. "I can't relax anymore. It's just too much for me."

Calmly he responded with, "Let me work with you first." For the next 15 minutes he stood next to the bed and took charge of the action. "Relax your forehead. Stop arching your back. Uncurl your toes. Take a cleansing breath. Now start the breathing. Focus. That's good. Keep it up."

With his help, I regained control of myself, and with his action-oriented response as a model, my husband was able to step in and keep me working effectively for the rest of my labor and on through the birth of our son an hour and a half later. I never received, nor did I miss, the Demerol I had originally requested.

My experience confirmed what has been said by many—that a mother's request for medication is often a request for help. This made me aware of the need for practical instruction—especially for expectant fathers—in how to cope when the going gets rough, not just for when things proceed as expected. I began to translate this awareness into action when I became a certified childbirth educator.

It is important to realize that a woman who panics during a contraction often feels, as I did, like a person who is drowning. The waves keep coming. It's hard to catch your breath. There seems to be no letup. Drowning persons do not wonder what their rescuers are feeling or what their qualifications are. They simply reach out and try to grab on. It is only necessary that the rescuer know what to do in order to make an effective rescue.

If your wife panics and says, "I don't know if I can handle the next one," she is asking for your help. In spite of how you may feel at that moment, there is a very effective sequence of actions you can take. I call it "the panic routine," and it consists of just a few simple steps:

1) *Stand Up*. This action says without words, "I'm here and I'm in charge." A husband is usually seated next to a high hospital bed, which invariably bring his eye level well beneath his wife's. By standing, he reverses the situation and thereby renders himself the authority. This simple act of *standing up* during the tough moments is probably the single most important action an expectant father can take during the time his wife is in labor.

2) *Grasp Her Wrist*. This sends the message, "I care about you. I'm not going to let you be swept away."

3) *Bombard Her Senses With Input.*

■ *Central vision:* Bring your face within ten inches of her face so she has no choice but to pay full attention to you.

■ *Peripheral vision:* Move your free hand up and down, off to the side of her face, to reinforce the breathing rhythm and rate.

■ *Audio:* Do your breathing with a loud, throaty sound—louder than hers so you will attract her attention.

In doing step #3, your aim is to engage her total attention. You start by doing whatever breathing pattern she is doing but louder and more vigorously, and then you lead her down to a slower, quieter, more rhythmic pace—using the breathing technique appropriate to her progress in labor. It is most important to *start where she is*, however irregular, fast, or noisy, rather than to start by doing what you think she should be doing.

If your wife refuses eye contact by turning her head from side to side as you bring your face close up to hers, then use both of your hands (give up wrist-holding and hand-waving) to grasp her face firmly, a hand on each cheek, and make her look at you. In this case you will have to rely on eye contact and audio input to lead her back into good breathing control. If she breaks away from your hands, simply grab her face again and hold on tight. This action says, "I'm strong, I care, you can regain control."

Although the procedure is very simple, it helps to try it out ahead of time. One day when the two of you are practicing the breathing techniques, have your wife act as if she were losing control. For example, she can make her breathing noisy or arrhythmic, or she can just stop doing the breathing technique midstream. Whenever you observe her doing any of these things, you go through "the panic routine."

During labor itself, observe your wife carefully. When she first shows signs of struggle during a contraction—her breathing may get noisier, or her body may move about in a restless or agitated fashion—stand up and breathe with her rather than wait until she loses control.

Following are the experiences of two different couples who were able to use "the panic routine" effectively:

First, Tony. "When I got into the labor area after Linda was admitted, I heard someone screaming. It was a shock to find out it was Linda. I thought she would be able to deal with labor after taking the course. The first thing I did was put my hands on her cheeks and my face up close to hers, and then I started going through the breathing with her because she was completely out of control. She responded to me. It took a lot of time because she would get control for a short while, and then another contraction would come that was more than the others, and she would lose it, and I would have to go through the same thing all over again. She finally started doing everything herself without any help when she was in transition. That's when she got the hang of it."

Now, Brenda. "I got panicky, but not so much panicky as I wanted to give up. Carlos felt I should keep on working, and he was right. He got me back on track. He stood right in front of me, and he had to stand in front of me in every direction because I was flailing all over the place at that point. He ran from side to side and made sure he did the breathing ten times as heavily as I was doing it, and he made sure I didn't look at anything but him. We had to work for half an hour that way. I responded to him. I can't believe I did. Carlos just made sure I had him in front of me all the time."

As you can see from the experiences of these couples, what you do is far more important than how you feel. Feel as you may during the experience, but *act* as the situation demands.

Pregnancy—
It's A Psychological Experience Too
by Dr. Elizabeth M. Whelan

Most of the popular books for expectant parents tell you everything you want to know about the biological aspects of pregnancy—the step-by-step growth of the fetus, the changes that occur in your body as it develops its capacity to nourish and protect your growing baby. But what is often understated is the equally dramatic psychological changes that occur during those all-important months. Certainly, each pregnancy is its own unique psychological experience, but it's clear that there are some distinct alterations during each and every pregnancy—both in you and your feelings and in your relationship with others.

Your Mixed Feelings

Do you remember the day you got the news? I certainly do! "Your test is positive, Mrs. Whelan; you're pregnant!" Despite the fact that we were scientifically planning the pregnancy, the confirmation still came as somewhat of a jolt. "Are you *sure?*" I kept asking the nurse over the phone. "Don't these tests often have some false positive results?" I gasped (knowing very well that false positives were very infrequent.)

On one hand I reacted with joy and wonder, projecting ahead a number of months to imagine what this newly created life would be like. And I was really very pleased I could conceive—after all, you never really know until you try. The first thing I did was pull out all my biology and physiology books. Suddenly the chapters on reproduction and the pictures of a three-week-old zygote (which I now feel is a cold, overly scientific term to describe *my* baby!) took on new meaning. "That's what my child looks like now," I would think as I shook my head in wonder.

But on the other hand, my reaction was not all positive. And in talking to other expectant new mothers, I found that my mixed feelings were not unique. "Although I was thrilled, I was apprehensive at the same time," Joan, a thirty-year old high school teacher in her ninth month, told me. "There was so much else going on in our lives right then. I had just started a new job, and we had just moved into a new house and had months of redecorating ahead of us. I began to question whether this was the most convenient time. And I was downright scared about the responsibility I had suddenly assumed. How did I know I could handle it? It was a bit late at that point to be asking questions, but I did wonder, 'Do I really want this baby?' ''

Ambivalence about being pregnant can manifest itself in a number of ways. Some women are simply unable to buy—or even look at—baby clothes during their early months. Others suffer periods of depression when they seriously regret that they are expecting a child. Studies have shown that early in pregnancy, as many as half of the women who enthusiastically planned the conception have serious second thoughts. And the percentage is much higher among those whose pregnancy "just happened."

So if you find yourself occasionally worried about your lack of enthusiasm, be aware that your reaction is fully normal. The mixed feelings may either suddenly disappear (for many, the event that dramatically shifts their attitude is quickening—the moment they start to feel the gentle flutter of life in their abdomen) or may gradually evolve to more positive thoughts. "When I was six months pregnant, I got to the point where I could *begin* looking at cribs," Emily, a mother of a four-month-old son, told me, "but I couldn't actually go to buy one until the eighth month! By that point, though, I could hardly wait until the crib had an occupant!"

The Highs And Lows

Pregnant women see and react to things differently than do nonpregnant women. (If you yourself haven't become convinced of this already, ask your husband!) What is technically known as "emotional liability," or frequent mood variation, is a psychological characteristic of the pregnant state, presumably a combined effect of the significant hormone surges you're experiencing, the sheer exhaustion you frequently feel, and the emotional burden that the awareness of impending parenthood carries with it.

Small family arguments, a minor exchange of harsh words which, in other circumstances would be quickly forgotten or ignored, can be enough to set off a flood of tears. "My husband made a sarcastic comment about the casserole I made last week," Sandra, in her fifth month of pregnancy, confided to me. "I immediately ran into the bedroom and cried for an hour. He didn't know what to do with me. And a few times during the last weeks, I've gotten very resentful that his life was proceeding as normal while my pace was slowing down. I've become a bit snappy, and when he responds in kind, I just collapse in tears."

Even if you *know* that you are emotionally vulnerable and tell yourself, "I'm overreacting because I'm pregnant," you can't always control the situation. But you can to some extent put things in perspective as the tears start to come.

The Changing You

"I was square and looked like a refrigerator approaching," was how humorist Jean Kerr described herself in the later stages of pregnancy. Obviously, the drastic change in your figure that occurs over the nine-month period is going to have some effect on your self-image.

At first, pregnancy can be just your secret—you can pass in your regular clothes. But eventually your bra and the buttons on your blouse begin to show the signs of strain, and the zipper on your skirt simply refuses to go up to the top. At this point your "psychological apparatus" may react to pregnancy in two ways: you might choose selectively from your regular wardrobe, or you might eagerly rush to your nearest maternity shop before you really need to. Some women are eager to reveal their condition to the world as soon as possible, walking with their shoulders rigidly back so their abdomen protrudes; others are more cautious about their public announcement. This difference in early reaction to physical changes of pregnancy is a matter of individual choice. But your reaction to body changes in the later months may be more significant.

Some women appear to be less than satisfied with themselves, especially in late pregnancy. "I think of maternity clothes as a uniform. You've got to wear them for your tour of duty," Anna, a twenty-year-old expectant mother said, "and even though my last months of pregnancy occurred in the hottest, driest months of the year, I always wore a raincoat when I went out—my attempt at disguise." Others seem to thoroughly enjoy seeing their abdomen expand. "I simply loved the way I looked when I was eight months pregnant," another new mother exclaimed to me. "I felt truly radiant and was proud of my bulging profile."

There's no denying that carrying around some unevenly distributed extra weight is not always comfortable, and not everyone constantly feels "radiant." But it is important in terms of a healthy psychological adjustment to come to terms with your changing body image and certainly not feel you have to hide it. By following the nutritional and exercise guidelines your doctor gives you, and by choosing flattering maternity clothes, you may indeed find that you *do* become radiant during your pregnancy and feel healthier than you have ever felt in your life.

Your Relationship With Others

From the moment you tell people you're pregnant, you may find them reacting differently to you. Some relationships may improve dramatically; others may appear threatened.

Your husband may be more solicitous of you, offering help and support at many times. Or he may be withdrawn, pensive, seemingly disturbed about your condition, attempting to cope with his own mixed feelings about becoming a father. (More likely, he will alternate, displaying both reactions.) You may find that your relationship with your relatives—particularly your mother and other female relatives with children of their own—improves simply because suddenly you have much more in common. On the other hand, you may experience more conflicts as you encounter ''self-appointed experts'' who offer endless advice on pregnancy, childbirth, and parenthood, or perhaps detect a bit of competition over who is or will be the better mother.

Perfect strangers may suddenly become very friendly, eager to offer you a seat on a crowded bus, patting your protruding abdomen as if it were public property. ''I met more people in the elevator of my apartment building during my last month of pregnancy than I had in the whole six years I'd lived there,'' one young mother exclaimed. ''Everyone had a comment or question about the expected baby.'' But your friends and business associates may surprise you. While some may be genuinely thrilled to hear your news, enthusiastically supporting your decision to have a child, others may be very cool.

''I was frankly astonished at the reaction of some of my business associates,'' one market research specialist complained. ''A number of my colleagues expressed a 'well-she's-pregnant-so-we-can't-count-on-her-anymore' attitude. I felt I had to work even harder during my pregnancy to prove that I was both capable and interested in my work.''

Pregnancy *is* accompanied by some psychological changes. Indeed these months add up to what psychiatrists call a ''developmental crisis,'' not necessarily a crisis in terms of tears and trauma but a crisis nonetheless. The transition from the status of non-parent to parent is not always an easy one. There will be some trying moments of confusion, conflict, anxiety, and perhaps mild depression. But by keeping aware of some of the normal changes you'll be dealing with—and staying attuned to some of the potential pitfalls—you'll weather your own personal ''developmental crisis'' and emerge with a new sense of self-esteem and self-confidence, having reoriented yourself in preparation for the responsibilities and rewards of parenthood.

New Options In Childbirth, Part 1
Family-Centered Maternity Care
by Myryame Montrose

Cheerful wallpaper brightens the room. Soft light filters through curtained windows. The stillness is broken by the rhythmic breathing of a woman in labor and the words of encouragement offered by her husband. Together in this cozy bedroom, they will welcome their baby into the world.

Until recently such a scenario could only have taken place at home, but this "cozy bedroom" is in fact a hospital room. The "birthing room" provides a homelike atmosphere for labor and delivery, but with ready access to equipment and facilities which might be needed. And now more and more hospitals will be offering options like the birthing room as part of their family-centered maternity care.

What Is Family-Centered Maternity Care?

Today we recognize that the birth of a baby is also the birth of a family. Each family member—mother, father, an older child—is profoundly affected by the addition of a new member. Ideally, each birth should draw the family unit closer together. Thus family-centered maternity care focuses on the physical, social, psychological and economic needs of the total family unit. One important way to facilitate these needs is to make the birth process accessible to as many family members as possible.

The desire to have family members participate fully in the birth is apparently so strong that more and more couples are choosing to give birth at home (often without any medical supervision). The home birth movement appears to be a protest against the cold, sterile surroundings and high-technology procedures that are routine in many hospitals. But home births pose many risks to mother and baby; last minute emergencies can crop up in even the most "normal" pregnancies. The majority of couples would probably agree with this mother's assessment of the problem: "If people could have whomever they wanted with them, more people might choose to deliver in a hospital, which I feel is safer than home.''

This option is rapidly becoming viable. In an effort to stem the rising tide of home births, medical organizations are urging a more liberal hospital policy. Last year the Interprofessional Task Force on Health Care of Women and Children proposed that hospitals adopt the following family-centered childbirth policies:

1) All hospitals should offer birth preparation classes for both mothers and fathers, including instruction on breast-feeding and the role men can play in delivery.

2) Fathers should be permitted to accompany women giving birth during the entire process, including being present in the delivery room and helping at the birth itself. There should be no restriction on this privilege if the two parents are not married.

3) Hospitals would offer parents the option of using a homelike ''birthing room'' rather than a standard delivery room. The birthing room would contain informal furnishings and bear little resemblance to a surgical facility, as delivery rooms now do.

4) There would be an end to restrictions—some spelled out by state law or health department regulation—on young children visiting their mothers and newborn siblings in the hospital.

5) Hospitals would develop programs to accelerate the release of mothers after birth, so the newborn and its mother could quickly move back to the more psychologically secure atmosphere of the home. Hospitals would probably have to develop programs in which health professionals visited mothers and new babies at home.

Virtually identical position papers were approved by the American College of Obstetrics and Gynecology, the American Academy of Pediatrics, the American College of Nurse-Midwives, and the American Nurses Association.

Although a few hospitals already offer such programs, widespread acceptance of these proposals would result in nothing short of a revolution in the way most American babies are born today.

The Impetus For Change

Many of our own mothers were completely ''knocked out'' for delivery while our fathers paced anxiously in the waiting room. Today we attend preparation for childbirth classes. We choose to be active participants in the birth process, often with our husband's assistance.

In our newly found expertise in childbirth, we owe a deep debt of gratitude to those who began to question birth procedures as far back as the 1930s. English obstetrician Grantly Dick-Read; Dr. Fernand Lamaze of France, and Sheila Kitzinger, a childbirth educator and herself the mother of five, all pioneered concepts of prepared childbirth which are still popular today.

Drs. Marshall Klaus and John Kennell, as well as other scientists, have shown us how important the process of parent-child bonding is to future parent-child relationships ("bonding" is the term for the mutual attachments formed by mother and baby at birth). It is primarily due to their findings that hospitals are now allowing parents time alone with their baby immediately after birth to make skin-to-skin and eye contact, which are crucial to the bonding process, rather than whisking the baby off to the newborn nursery.

And more and more hospitals have begun to incorporate some of the delivery room procedures (dim lights, a hushed atmosphere, a warm water bath for the newborn) advocated by Dr. Frederick Leboyer, who claims that these procedures help ease the newborn's traumatic entry into the world.

Along with these new insights into birth have come consumer demands for a more satisfying, personalized birth experience. And as consumers become more knowledgeable, their priorities take on more weight with the medical community.

Last January, for example, Diana Korte and Roberta Scaer, M.S.W., of Boulder, Colorado, surveyed nearly 700 mothers in their community on their priorities for maternity care. Armed with a small grant from a local chapter of the March of Dimes, their immediate goal was to provide the local Community Hospital with consumer feedback it might use in planning its new maternity wing. Although the respondents came from three different groups (La Leche League, childbirth training classes, and a random sampling of new mothers), they were unanimous in selecting the options of having fathers present in labor and delivery rooms as the most important. They also felt fathers should have unrestricted visiting rights. And they had strong feelings about many other childbirth options. For example, 90 percent of the mothers in the La Leche Group felt that it was very important to be able to initiate breast-feeding within an hour after birth. (Community Hospital in Boulder later agreed to offer most of the services or options the women had asked for.)

The new sibling visitation program at Stanford University Hospital in California is another example of how dialogue between consumers and hospitals can bring about changes in maternity care. This past December the hospital announced that children would be allowed to visit their newborn brothers and sisters in the maternity unit. The new policy (which began, fittingly, on Christmas Eve) allows children to view the newborn through the nursery window and also to visit with mother and newborn in the mother's room. The Birth Action Council, a group of parents who had given birth at Stanford, assisted the hospital in drawing up the new policy. Suzanne Arms, author of the book *Immaculate Deception,* a searing indictment of modern hospital birth practices, is one of the members of the Council. She hailed the new visitation policy as "a recognition of the fact that all births are primarily family events."

The increasingly high price of giving birth in a hospital (perhaps as much as $1,200, not including the physician's fees) has been another impetus for change, as consumers and hospital administrators alike look for ways to reduce costs. Obstetricians who specialize in coping with high-risk patients; expensive technology and equipment, and the cost of a lengthy postpartum stay, may not be necessary in handling the births of low-risk patients.

Putting Family-Centered Concepts Into Practice

A handful of hospitals and alternate birth centers have developed innovative programs to provide birthing couples with individualized care. For example, in 1964 Roosevelt Hospital instituted its nurse-midwifery service. By making nurse-midwives an integral part of the obstetrical team, they hoped to provide a model for the rest of the country to follow. In 1975 the nurse-midwifery service became available for private patients. The staff of Certified Nurse Midwives (graduate nurses with extra training in labor and delivery), directed by Barbara Brennan, CNM, offers a complete maternity care package for low-risk patients, combining medical expertise with psychological support.

A woman who is enrolled in the nurse-midwifery service at Roosevelt will see her midwife during the prenatal period, have her full support during labor and delivery, and return for a postnatal checkup. The midwives are fully qualified to handle all aspects of a normal birth, yet should the need arise, doctors and emergency equipment are immediately available. At Roosevelt fathers (or anyone else the mother chooses) are encouraged to participate in labor and delivery; parents and new baby are given time alone after birth to get acquainted; fathers may visit at any time, and rooming-in is available.

Although Roosevelt does not offer a homelike setting for birth (plans for a new birthing room are under discussion), Dr. Thomas F. Dillon, Director of Roosevelt's Ob/Gyn Service, feels that companionship and support during birth are more important than plants and decor. "Ambiance," he notes, "is not just how the walls are painted.'' (Average fee for the nurse-midwifery service is about $900.)

Across town at the Maternity Center Association's Child-bearing Center, which opened in 1975, the emphasis is on home-style births. The surroundings play an important role by creating a homelike atmosphere. Located in a former townhouse, the Child-bearing Center has two labor/delivery bedrooms cheerfully decorated and furnished with a large, comfortable bed, an overstuffed lounge chair, and other homey touches. There are also a family room and a garden which couples may use during the early stages of labor. The woman may choose whom she wishes to have with her for the birth, and afterwards father and other children may witness the newborn's physical examination. In most cases the new family is on its way home within 12 hours of the birth.

The Child-bearing Center is staffed with certified nurse-midwives (and back-up physicians), who aim to give each couple as much control as possible over the delivery of their child. Since the Center is equipped only to handle ''normal'' births, candidates are rigorously screened for medical risks. Should an emergency arise, the back-up hospital is just 15 blocks away. Though some medical authorities would argue that even this distance (an eleven-minute ambulance trip in heavy traffic) is too great in an emergency, the Center has not yet had to make any emergency transfers involving a life-threatening situation.

The Child-bearing Center was conceived as a model facility to show that low-risk pregnancies need not be treated in a traditional hospital setting, and as a way to ''bring back into the system those families who had lost trust and refused to go to the hospital.'' For hundreds of couples, it has done just that. (The fee for prenatal, delivery and postpartum care is $850.)

Booth Maternity Center in Philadelphia (a Salvation Army-based maternity hospital for low- and moderate-risk patients) has many features in common with the M.C.A. Child-bearing Center. Here, too, a small team of nurse-midwives and obstetricians focuses on pregnancy as a normal physiological event. The family-centered program was begun in 1971 under the direction of John B. Franklin. The Center has always offered parents options and encouraged them to articulate their desires for the birth environment and methods of treatment, and they hope to have home-style birthing suites in the near future. In its handbook for patients, the Center describes its aims as follows: ''At Booth we are dedicated to the belief that bringing a new baby into the world can be a celebration for the entire family in an atmosphere of joy and dignity. Your experience is unique. Our aim is to make it comfortable and rewarding.'' (Average cost of maternity care at Booth is $1,350, including physicians' fees.)

Mount Zion Hospital's Alternative Birth Center in San Francisco has provided a "home birth" experience, within the hospital framework since May 1976. Two comfortable rooms have been set aside (with plans for a third to open soon), each one decorated with rugs, stereo, wallhangings and plants. The bed is large enough to accommodate both mother and father, and there is also a couch for other visitors. The actual delivery takes place right there in that bed, so the mother doesn't have to be moved from labor room to delivery room to recovery room (being moved during a labor contraction can be very uncomfortable).

An obstetrical nurse remains with the family throughout the labor period, and the delivery is attended by the woman's private obstetrician or one of the hospital's obstetrical staff. Older children may be present for the birth for as long as parents want them there, and that goes for grandparents as well. Once the baby is born, the newborn is never taken from the mother unless complications make it necessary. The mother stays at the hospital a minimum of six hours (and usually less than 48 hours). A nurse will visit the new family twice within 72 hours after birth, the first time within 24 hours.

As in most alternate birth programs, mothers are carefully screened, and the parents-to-be must have attended natural birth classes beforehand. At the Alternate Birth Center, a delivery costs only $400 (not including doctors' fees), versus $1,000 at Mount Zion's conventional facility. This lower cost reflects the fact that an A.B.C. mother does not use the hospital's labor room and nursery and is usually on the premises less than 48 hours.

Mount Zion's Alternate Birth Center was the brainchild of Dr. Roberta Ballard, chief of pediatrics and director of the A.B.C. She came up with the idea after the birth of her own child at the hospital, five years ago. In her opinion, "A 'home birth' experience is probably better for both the baby and the mother, when there are no obvious problems, and if it takes place in the safe environment of a hospital."

And there are many other examples of how hospitals are turning conventional maternity departments into "home birthing" facilities. Family Hospital in Milwaukee established its Life Center for Maternity Care in 1972. Its slogan, "Preparation for a New Life," is directed toward families as well as their babies. "We are mindful," says Executive Director Walter G. Hardin, "that parents, not nurses and doctors, are having the baby." The patient maintains as many controls as possible, and the environment is homelike and comfortable.

The Birth Center at Forest Grove Community Hospital in Oregon provides several options for parents including delivery by a nurse-midwife, husband coached childbirth, Leboyer births, as well as rooming-in. The labor/birth room is decorated with personal touches to make the family feel at home, and birthing attendants are encouraged to act as if The Birth Center belongs to the family during their stay.

At St. Joseph Hospital in Stamford, Connecticut, there are two Lamaze labor-delivery rooms equipped with specially designed labor-delivery beds imported from France. The Lamaze rooms have been decorated to achieve a homelike atmosphere and have personal amenities such as soft lighting, a telephone, radio and private bath. And there is a special family room where older children may visit with mother and view baby through the nursery window.

Memorial Hospital in Phoenix, Arizona, opened a home-style birthing room two years ago. It was the first hospital in Phoenix to allow fathers in the delivery room; now it has also become the first to allow friends and relatives to watch the birth. Here, too, the decor of the birthing room is similar to a bedroom at home.

At Booth Memorial Hospital in Cleveland, families can move into one of four apartment-like suites (located in a building immediately adjacent to the hospital) and give birth in a homey environment. The average stay is 24 hours with follow-up care provided at home by a staff member.

Franklin Square Hospital in Baltimore, Maryland, plans to open new maternity facilities this spring. There will be six combination labor/delivery rooms, decorated to achieve a relaxed setting, and six alternate-birth rooms, similarly decorated, but with a difference. The alternate-birth rooms, reserved for low-risk patients, will not have emergency equipment in the rooms themselves. Of course, in an emergency, necessary equipment would be within a few feet. Both rooms will feature a new bed designed by the hospital's ob/gyn staff.

Highland Park Hospital in Illinois recently opened a new maternity-family lounge where siblings can visit their mother. By stepping up on the special viewing bench, children can take a peek at the baby through the nursery window. Now Highland Park Hospital has petitioned the state for permission to open the first birthing room in the area. If the plan is approved, the room should be in operation by July of this year.

Thanks to the initiatives of these institutions (and others like them throughout the country), parents have been given a choice about where and how they'd like their baby to be born. And the success of such family-centered maternity care seems certain to inspire more options for the future. Although the details of individual family-centered childbirth programs may vary widely even within a given community, they all have one goal in mind: to make birth a family affair.

New Options In Childbirth, Part 2
Family-Centered Cesarean Births
by Myryame Montrose

The man at the head of the operating table smiles at the woman being prepared for a Cesarean delivery. She is grateful for the presence and support of this man dressed in surgical cap, gown and mask—and gives her husband's hand a gentle squeeze. The important thing, she thinks, is not how their baby will be born but the fact that they will share the experience together.

In a few hospitals scenes like this one are already taking place. And with increased consumer demand for family-centered births to include the Cesarean couple, it's likely that husband-attended Cesareans will be more common in the future.

Another Way To Have A Baby

Today many parents-to-be take classes to prepare for an active role in childbirth. Hospitals have developed family-centered maternity programs to make the birth process truly a family event. But often this shared birth experience is denied the Cesarean couple, who may feel they have been "cheated" out of their baby's birth. The woman who has prepared for childbirth by taking special classes may think that she has "flunked the final" by not being able to deliver vaginally; her husband often feels "left out and let down." Sensitive doctors and childbirth instructors have been surprised, and somewhat horrified, to learn that so many Cesarean couples have strong negative feelings about the experience which can carry over to other areas of their relationship and influence their attitude towards the baby, if left unresolved.

But we are learning that by changing hospital policies to allow couples to remain together, and by providing education and support, a Cesarean can be a positive birth experience.

To begin with, we must recognize that a Cesarean is primarily a *birth* and not just another operation. Some hospitals no longer use the term Cesarean-section (which places the emphasis on the surgical procedure) but instead use phrases such as abdominal birth or Cesarean delivery to underscore the birth aspect. There is also a danger in referring to vaginal deliveries as "normal" or "natural," thereby implying that there is something wrong with having a Cesarean. In fact, this may be the only way to assure the birth of a healthy baby in some cases.

Why A Cesarean?

Not so long ago a Cesarean was considered a last resort delivery method, and hospitals judged the quality of their obstetric care in terms of a low Cesarean rate. Today, however, the procedure is much safer due to advances in surgical technique and anesthesia, and many doctors feel that a Cesarean delivery is preferable to subjecting a baby to a difficult vaginal birth. A traumatic birth, they point out, can have long-lasting effects on a child's physical and mental development.

This concern with the quality of a baby's condition at birth, and the availability of sophisticated new medical techniques that can alert doctors to signs of fetal distress, are the major reasons for the increase in Cesarean deliveries. Fear of malpractice suits has also helped drive Cesarean rates up. In 1970 only 5% of American babies were delivered by Cesarean; now the average rate is estimated at 10-15%, with reports of over 20% at some hospitals (particularly for large teaching hospitals, which tend to see more high-risk patients).

In other words, one out of every ten pregnant women in the United States today can anticipate a Cesarean birth.

There are many reasons why a doctor may decide to do a Cesarean. For example, the baby's head may be too large to fit through the birth canal *(cephalo-pelvic disproportion)*. The placenta may separate from the uterine wall prior to delivery, thus cutting off the fetal supply of nutrients *(placenta abruptio)*. Or if the placenta precedes the baby and lies over the cervical *os* or opening at the mouth of the uterus *(placenta previa)*, there is danger of maternal hemorrhage cutting off the baby's oxygen supply. A Cesarean may also be indicated because of the mother's medical history. Diabetes, high blood pressure, Rh incompatibility, and toxemia of pregnancy can all pose a threat to both mother and baby. In such cases the doctor may want to deliver the baby before the actual due date, either by induction of labor and/or Cesarean. And because most doctors in this country believe in the policy "once a Cesarean, always a Cesarean," for fear of possible uterine rupture, a woman who delivers a baby by Cesarean will probably have any additional children the same way. Although some doctors disagree with this policy, repeat Cesareans account for a large portion of the total figures.

The use of fetal monitoring equipment during labor can help doctors follow a baby's progress and alert them to changes in his condition which may signal *fetal distress.* A slow heart rate may mean that something has gone wrong—the umbilical cord may have become twisted, for example. Signs of fetal distress are usually considered an indication for immediate Cesarean, unless a vaginal delivery is imminent.

And at most hospitals, indications for routine Cesareans have been broadened to include instances where the baby's head is not in the usual head first position for birth *(malpresentation),* particularly if this is a first baby. When a baby is lying crosswise in the womb *(transverse)* or in *breech* position (feet and/or buttocks first), many doctors feel a Cesarean delivery is preferable to trying to turn the baby around or attempting a difficult forceps delivery, which might injure the child.

Critics point out that in deciding to do a Cesarean, possible benefits to the baby must be weighed against potential risks for the mother. For while Cesareans are considered to be one of the safest surgical procedures, they are still not so safe as a vaginal delivery. Although maternal deaths due to Cesareans have been virtually eliminated, the risk of complications is nearly three times higher for women who deliver by Cesarean. Possible complications include hemorrhage, serious infections, blood clots and injury to the bladder or intestines.

However, there is some risk involved in any type of birth. And most women who have delivered by Cesarean are thankful that this technique has allowed them to have a healthy baby. What they would like, in addition, is a way to make this type of birth a less frightening and more fulfilling way to have a baby.

"If Only We Could Have Been Together"

Most hospitals now use regional anesthetics (such as a spinal block) for Cesareans, so the mother is awake during the operation. But in many hospitals, there is no one by her side during the procedure to offer comfort and support — the medical staff is too busy delivering the baby. This would seem to be an ideal role for the father. In talking to Cesarean couples, over and over again I heard the comment, "If only we could have been together."

Gail and Billy C. had taken Lamaze classes and eagerly anticipated the birth of their first baby. Three weeks before her due date, Gail discovered that a Cesarean was likely because her baby was in breech position. When their childbirth instructor learned that a Cesarean might be necessary, she spent a lesson discussing the operation, so Gail and Billy felt prepared. They were not prepared, however, for the disappointment and fear they felt upon being separated. Billy later admitted that while Gail was in the operating room (a total of perhaps 45 minutes), he'd felt more afraid than he ever had before, including the two years he'd spent in Vietnam. Both agree that any fears would have been banished if they could have been together.

Family-Centered Cesareans

Keeping the family together for the momentous occasion of birth is what family-centered maternity care is all about. Though programs vary from hospital to hospital, key factors are usually 1) prenatal education for birth; 2) husband-attended childbirth; 3) an opportunity for the new family to spend time alone together after the birth (both to foster bonding and so the mother can begin breast-feeding, if she wishes); 4) a liberal visiting policy that allows fathers to come as often as they like, and some provision for visits by other children in the family.

Now there are a few hospitals throughout the country which offer family-centered care for Cesarean couples. One such hospital is Community General in Reading, Pennsylvania.

According to Dr. J. Robert McTammany, head of obstetrics and gynecology at Community General, husband-attended Cesareans began several years ago when one father (who had prepared for a Lamaze delivery) just assumed that he could still be with his wife when a Cesarean became necessary. And Dr. McTammany couldn't think of any medical reason why the father shouldn't be admitted. Thus began a policy that is now upheld by the hospital's bylaws: "Cesarean-section is an operation, but it is still fundamentally a childbirth and the family should be together." In fact, says Dr. McTammany, "At Community General we feel the most important part of the entire childbirth process is the welcome the baby gets into the world. You can't imagine the beauty of seeing the mother, father and baby, in the midst of all the bustle in the operating room, tune out the whole thing and just concentrate on each other." This close interaction after birth fosters parent-child bonding, which we now know is a critical factor in getting a family off to a good start.

Although most hospitals do not allow fathers to be present if the mother has been given a general anesthetic, Dr. McTammany points out that if the mother is asleep, the sole responsibility for bonding rests with the father. By allowing the father to be present when the mother is asleep, he can become her "eyes and ears" for the birth and help her recapture something of the experience she has missed. (Dr. McTammany also encourages the father to take pictures of the newborn, which he can later share with his wife.)

Janet N. confirms that having a husband's support is important, even if you are not awake for the Cesarean. "Our first experience was at a rather large hospital in California. Richard was not allowed to watch. The experience was miserable for both of us...all because of rules and regulations and the feeling the doctors didn't want to be bothered.'' Since Janet is an x-ray technologist and has herself taught childbirth classes, she was careful to plan the type of experience she wanted for her next Cesarean. ''The second birth,'' she explains, ''took place in a small town in Colorado. The doctors agreed to let Richard attend. I knew ahead of time I would be having general anesthesia. If I couldn't see the birth of our child, at least Richard could. I remember waking up on the operating table ...the look on his face told the whole story.'' But as Janet points out, ''If it wasn't for my medical experience and forwardness with our doctors, where would we have been? Frightened! There need to be more reading materials and openness on the subject of Cesareans. This is not a horrid or ugly experience; this is the birth of your baby.''

The Need For Education And Support

Preparation for childbirth can be an important factor in making birth a positive experience, but traditional childbirth classes do not adequately prepare couples for a Cesarean. Now Cesarean couples can find classes and support groups geared to their special needs.

Ruth Allen, a British-trained nurse-midwife, and Bonnie Donovan, a childbirth educator, have worked closely over the past four years to improve care for Cesarean families. As head nurse in labor and delivery at South Shore Hospital in Massachusetts, Ms. Allen was concerned about the negative reactions of parents whose babies had been delivered by emergency Cesarean. She set up a discussion group for Cesarean parents to determine what kinds of information and support were needed.

As a result of these discussions, Ruth Allen and Bonnie Donovan developed the first curriculum for Cesarean preparation classes in 1974. The series of classes they designed, called the Cesarean Birth Method, has served as a model for similar courses at other hospitals.

The special Cesarean course is geared to couples who anticipate this type of delivery (in addition, information on Cesarean births is included in all child-birth classes). The series of four classes covers in detail: the operation itself, including information on types of anesthesia, incisions, and what types of sensations to expect; a discussion of various tests that may be performed to determine the baby's well-being during pregnancy or to determine the fetus' age in order to avoid a premature delivery; a discussion of the father's role if he is to share the birth; a tour of the hospital's obstetric facilities; a slide presentation of a Cesarean birth, and information on postpartum recovery and child care. Relaxation breathing techniques are also taught, which can be helpful in alleviating pain. In addition to practical information, the classes stress the fact that a Cesarean can be just as joyful as any other type of delivery.

Since 1976 South Shore has permitted fathers who have taken the Cesarean course to be present at the birth. "It's nice to see fathers come out of a Cesarean birth full of the joy and wonder of childbirth," notes Ms. Allen. "It is a *birth*, not just an operation." The hospital takes a picture of the baby being delivered to show father and mother (as at most hospitals, a screen is placed across the mother's head and shoulders to hold the sterile drapes used during the operation; thus the parents do not actually watch the procedure).

Bonnie Donovan now teaches Cesarean classes at the Jordan Hospital in Plymouth, Massachusetts (she's had two children by Cesarean herself and is the author of *The Cesarean Birth Experience*). These classes, she explains, not only give parents confidence but also help make the baby's birth and the transition to parenthood easier, both physically and emotionally. "The differences between couples who have not been to class and those who have are often remarkable. The ones who attend classes usually have a far better birth experience," she notes.

Judith Gunderson, R.N., who coordinates parent education classes at Boston Hospital for Women, agrees. "After the Cesarean those who attended classes evaluate the course and write a commentary on their birth experience. Evaluations of the course are always very positive, and those women who had their partner with them in the operating room comment on the importance of being together and how much it meant to them."

In addition to preparation for the Cesarean, there is also a need for support after the baby is born. Even when the birth itself is a good experience, a woman who has had a Cesarean may feel guilty if she is not up to caring for her baby to the same degree that she might after an easy vaginal delivery. It can be reassuring for her to learn that her recovery rate is similar to that of other Cesarean mothers. After all, she must recover not only from a birth but also from major surgery. And if the birth experience was not a good one, she may have to deal with feelings of loss or anger or guilt, as well.

A number of groups have been formed in recent years to provide just this type of moral support. Often they have begun as a simple rap group of two or three mothers who get together to share their experiences and investigate ways they can help change the "system." Karen Barth, who now teaches Cesarean classes in the Reading area, started such a discussion group after her first, deeply disappointing Cesarean delivery. She points out that in addition to having "lost" the birth experience, many women are made to feel guilty about their disappointment. After all, they do have a healthy baby, why dwell on the birth itself?

Perhaps, as Karen suggests, the process of giving birth is a necessary psychological completion to pregnancy, and the experience of giving birth an important factor in the transition from pregnancy to motherhood.

The point of family-centered Cesarean care is to return the birth experience to the family. The success of such programs is proof that a Cesarean can be handled in such a way as to provide families with a joyful birth experience.

Where To Go For Help

Additional information about Cesareans can be obtained from the following groups:

C/SEC (Cesareans/Support, Education and Concern), 66 Christopher Road, Waltham, Massachusetts 02154. (Write for information about groups in your area; ask for publications list.)

Cesarean Birth Council, 1402 Nilde Avenue, Mountain View, California 94040. (Information on groups throughout California; classes, pamphlets and films on Cesareans.)

ASPO (American Society for Psychoprophylaxis in Obstetrics), 1411 K Street NW, Washington, D.C. 20005.

I.C.E.A. (International Childbirth Education Association), P.O. Box 20048, Minneapolis, Minnesota 55420. (Both ASPO and I.C.E.A. can provide information about local childbirth classes and Cesarean support groups.)

Additional Reading

The Cesarean Birth Experience, A Practical, Comprehensive and Reassuring Guide for Parents and Professionals, by Bonnie Donovan; Beacon Press (hardcover, $8.95; quality paperback, $4.95).

Having a Cesarean Baby, by Richard Hausknecht, M.D., and Joan R. Heilman; Dutton (paperback, $4.95).

The Modern Midwife
by Phyllis Evans

The word midwife suggests an old "granny" with a bottle of herbs in her back pocket, who helped nature run its course and hoped for the best. But today's certified nurse-midwife has quite a different image.

Cradling her newborn daughter, Heather, in her arms, Lillie Huey reflected on her childbirth experience. Less than 24 hours before, she had given birth to Heather without the use of medications or routine procedures such as IVs or episiotomies. Labor and delivery took place in a hospital birthing room decorated with a cheerful bedspread and curtains, a rocking chair, and a wicker table overflowing with plants. An obstetrician was not present at the birth; instead Lillie was guided through labor and delivery by her husband and the helping hands of another highly trained professional—a certified nurse-midwife.

"The experience was wonderful," says Lillie. "I felt comfortable and relaxed, and it seemed natural to have a woman helping with the delivery."

Like Lillie Huey, an increasing number of women who want undrugged, prepared childbirth, are seeking the services of a certified nurse-midwife for prenatal care through labor and delivery—care traditionally provided in this country by an obstetrician.

The word midwife (which in Old English literally means "with the woman") suggests an old "granny" with a bottle of herbs in her back pocket, who helped nature run its course and hoped for the best. But today's certified nurse-midwife has quite a different image.

What Is A Certified Nurse-Midwife?

According to the American College of Nurse-Midwives, the professional organization for nurse-midwives in the United States, "The nurse-midwife is a registered nurse who, by virtue of added knowledge and skill gained through an organized program of study and clinical experience, has extended the limits of her practice into the area of management of the care of mothers and babies throughout the maternity cycle so long as progress meets criteria accepted as normal."

This means that a certified nurse-midwife is an expert in handling normal pregnancies and deliveries. She cares for the pregnant woman during pregnancy and stays with her during labor and delivery, providing continuous physical and emotional support and watching for any signs that may require intervention by an obstetrician. She evaluates and provides immediate care for the newborn and after delivery helps the mother care for herself and her newborn, conducts a postpartum checkup, and counsels her patients on family planning.

The certified nurse-midwife is an important member of the hospital obstetric health care team, but she is never an independent practitioner. She always works in association with an obstetrician in case of any complications or medical emergencies.

To become a certified nurse-midwife, a woman must be a registered nurse and attend one of the 25 nationally approved educational programs in midwifery. Midwifery students can follow two courses of study: 1) the basic midwifery course, which results in a certificate and varies in length from nine to 12 months, or 2) for those who have bachelor's degrees, a one- to two-year program that results in a certificate along with a master's degree. Several midwifery programs offer internships for graduates who want more clinical experience before taking a job, and some programs also offer refresher courses for midwives who have been trained in other countries or who have not practiced in the last five years. By the time a nurse-midwife finishes her training, she will have performed a minimum of 20 deliveries and newborn examinations and conducted at least 20 first visits of pregnant women. After passing a rigorous national certification test prepared by the American College of Nurse-Midwives, she can use the initials C.N.M. (certified nurse-midwife) after her name. There are 2,100 C.N.M.s in the United States, 1,700 of whom are members of the American College of Nurse-Midwives. The profession is almost exclusively female, but there are currently 15 male C.N.M.s.

From Grannies To Graduates

Until the late nineteenth century in this country, babies were delivered by granny midwives. Then obstetrics became a medical specialty, and male physicians began to take over the care of the pregnant woman. At that time mortality rates for mothers and infants were extremely high, and women were urged to deliver their babies in hospitals, where "modern" techniques like anesthesia and forceps could be used.

The granny midwives were soon forced out of business, and in some states they were even outlawed. In 1905, for example, more than 40 percent of the babies born in New York were delivered by midwives; in 1906, the New York City Health Department condemned midwives; and by 1932 midwives delivered only about ten percent of all babies born in New York City. More and more states began to outlaw midwives, although they continued to (and still do) deliver 80 percent of the babies in the world.

Modern midwifery began in this country in 1925 when Mary Breckinridge, a public health nurse, started the Frontier Nursing Service midwifery program in rural Kentucky. Mary had attended an accredited midwifery program in England, and she brought British nurse-midwives to the U.S. and urged women to go to England for midwifery education and training. Her service in the mountainous backwoods of Kentucky spurred the resurgence of midwifery in the United States.

For the first time nurses were trained as nurse-midwives, and in 1955, the American College of Nurse-Midwives was formed to set the guidelines for accredited educational programs and to organize standards. However, nurse-midwives still faced fierce opposition from doctors and nurses who felt that only physicians could properly provide care for the pregnant woman and deliver her baby. It was not until 1971, when a joint statement was issued by the American College of Obstetricians and Gynecologists, their nurses' association, and the American College of Nurse-Midwives, that nurse-midwives gained acceptance among the medical profession.

The statement said that as part of a medically directed health-care team, "qualified nurse-midwives may assume responsibility for the complete care and management of uncomplicated maternity patients." With this vote of confidence from the medical establishment, a certified nurse-midwife finally became an important member of the obstetric health care team.

What Nurse-Midwives Offer

"We offer more personalized care, and unlike obstetricians, nurse-midwives do not have any other obligations," says Barbara Brennan, C.N.M., director of the Nurse-Midwifery Service at Roosevelt Hospital in New York City and author (with Joan Rattner Heilman) of *The Complete Book of Midwifery* (E.P. Dutton & Co., $4.95 paperback).

Like Mary Breckinridge, Barbara is one of the pioneers of modern midwifery in the U.S. She was hired in 1964 to help doctors at Roosevelt Hospital handle the overwhelming load of clinic patients and thereby became one of the first certified nurse-midwives to work in a hospital.

In fact, it was Dr. Ralph W. Gause, one of *American Baby*'s contributing editors, who encouraged Barbara to seek midwifery training. During a routine delivery at New York Hospital, where Barbara was a head nurse of labor and delivery and Dr. Gause was an attending physician, he turned to Barbara and said, "Why do we need doctors to handle normal deliveries? With some specialized training, you could do just as well.'' This casual comment led Barbara to attend the midwifery program at Downstate Medical Center in Brooklyn, New York, then one of the three existing programs in the country.

During her first ten years at Roosevelt, Barbara and four other certified nurse-midwives worked exclusively with clinic patients. But in the 1970s attitudes about childbirth had begun to change. Women no longer wanted pregnancy to be treated as an illness, and they demanded unmedicated, natural births. Well-educated, well-informed middle-class women began to view the certified nurse-midwife as an alternative to the obstetrician, and in 1975, Barbara and the other nurse-midwives at Roosevelt Hospital set up the first autonomous midwifery service for private patients in this country. They were immediately swamped with applicants; since then numerous private midwifery practices have been formed nationwide.

Says Barbara: ''The couples who come to us want a more active role in childbirth. They are highly motivated, well-informed about pregnancy, and they know what kind of birth experience they want.''

''I decided to become a patient at Roosevelt Hospital's Nurse-Midwifery Service after an obstetrician told me that he guaranteed a painless childbirth,'' says Lillie Huey. ''I wanted to be prepared for childbirth, not knocked out. And I certainly knew it wouldn't be painless.''

At Roosevelt Hospital, private patients receive a complete maternity care package for $1,179, which includes prenatal care through delivery, a post-partum checkup, and a two-day hospital stay. In comparison, an obstetrician's fee alone can be as high as $750 to $1,100.

''It's the little things that they do, like calling your mother after the baby is born, that make the birth so joyful,'' says Irene Devlin, a registered nurse whose two children have been delivered by midwives at Downstate Medical Center in Brooklyn, New York.

Joanne Middleton, C.N.M., director of Nurse-Midwifery Associates, which was formed in 1969, explains how their program works.

''Only women in good physical health expecting to have a healthy, normal birth are accepted into the program,'' she says. After an orientation visit to discuss what type of birth a couple wants and the nurse-midwives' own philosophies, a woman sees the three midwives on a rotating basis. By the time she is ready to deliver, she knows all of them.

If any complications develop during the course of a woman's pregnancy, she is

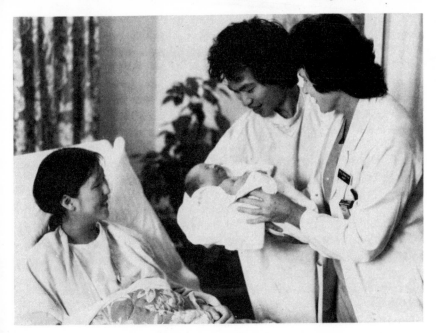

referred to one of the obstetricians who work in consultation with the midwifery service. "But we offer continuity of care," says Joanne. Even if a woman has to be transferred out of the program for medical reasons, the nurse-midwives still keep in touch and follow the progress of her pregnancy.

A woman in labor is met at the hospital by a nurse-midwife, who stays with her throughout labor and delivery. Enemas, shaves, and episiotomies are not done routinely at Downstate, and fetal monitors and IVs are rarely used. A woman is allowed to walk around during labor, and 70 percent of the deliveries take place right in the labor room.

All of the patients take preparation for childbirth classes taught by the nurse-midwives. Fathers are actively involved in the delivery; they often cut and clamp the umbilical cord.

"About 90 percent of our patients choose not to have medication," says Joanne. "The presence of the husband and a nurse-midwife, who encourages and guides her through the difficult stages of labor, often eliminates the need for drugs," adds Joanne.

Immediately after the delivery, mother, father, and baby are allowed time to get to know each other and form their first attachments, called bonding. Breast-feeding, rooming-in, and sibling visitations are all encouraged. In addition, the nurse-midwives at Downstate conduct follow-up parenting classes for parents of babies up to four months old.

Out-of-Hospital Births

Ironically, the current consumer demand for homestyle births has taken some certified nurse-midwives out of the hospital and back into the home.

One out-of-hospital birth alternative, run by certified nurse-midwives with the backup help of obstetricians, is the Child-bearing Center of the Maternity Center Association in New York City. Opened in 1975, the Center offers complete prenatal care through delivery. Labor/birth rooms resemble cozy bedrooms, and there's a family room and even a kitchen for those allowed at the birth. Patients are often discharged as soon as 12 hours after the birth. If any complications arise during labor, a woman is transferred to an obstetrician's care and taken to Lenox Hill Hospital, an 11-minute trip by ambulance.

"There's no reason why a healthy woman can't have her baby at home," says Lea Rizack, a certified nurse-midwife whose midwifery service is called Birth Options. Lea performs about 50 to 60 deliveries in the New York and New Jersey areas, both in and out of hospital. "There's a great demand for home deliveries, and I believe in them," says Lea, who works independently but has privileges at area hospitals. All of Lea's clients have backup obstetricians; her fee is based on what her clients can afford.

Lea was one of two certified nurse-midwives present at the birth of Sadie Ratliff's son, Garette. "We knew we wanted to have the baby at home; we wanted it to be our birth, and it was wonderful," says Sadie.

As her delivery date approached, the nurse-midwives called her to see how she was feeling. They visited her home to get to know her husband and other children and to become familiar with the surroundings. When she went into labor, a backup physician was notified in case of any complications. After the delivery the nurse-midwives stayed to help her husband clean up and to make sure that the entire family was comfortable, a practice common in Europe. A nurse-midwife came to visit the family the next day and then again three days after the birth. "That's when new mothers need the most reassurance," says Sadie. "It's so nice and so comforting to be told that you are doing OK."

It's those little extra touches—a few words of encouragement during labor and a follow-up phone call—that have made certified nurse-midwives so popular. Women are once again helping women give birth, allowing obstetricians to concentrate on high-risk cases. The result is better quality maternity care for all women in this country.

Chapter 2
The Care and Feeding of Baby

The Intensive Care Nursery, Part 1

by Dr. Ralph W. Gause

When Sarah was born, she was two months ahead of schedule. Frighteningly small and fragile, she weighed less than 1 1/2 pounds and could be cradled in one hand. She was struggling for life. Her breathing was shallow and erratic, and her digestive system was too immature to tolerate food. But Sarah was a fighter. She spent the first three months of her life in an intensive care nursery, and thanks to the care she received there, is a completely normal toddler today.

One of the authentic miracles of our time is that now even the sickest newborns have a good chance to grow up healthy. Twenty years ago hope was all but nonexistent for babies like Sarah. Many died a few hours after birth. Thousands of others never lived to see their first birthday. Still more grew up retarded or handicapped.

Today the lifesaving supports of the intensive care nursery (ICN) provide an environment in which sick newborns can be saved from damage or death. As part of its goal to improve the outcome of pregnancy and prevent birth defects, The March of Dimes Birth Defects Foundation supports many ICNs with funds for equipment and staff. When a baby at risk is brought to an ICN, results are dramatic. Four years ago, a newborn weighing less than 2-1/2 pounds had, at best, a 20 percent chance of survival. Today the chances are more than double that, and the babies are not merely surviving, but surviving undamaged in an encouraging number of cases.

With early intervention of ICN measures, which prevent high-risk factors from going unchecked, sick newborns have a healthier growth and development than would otherwise be possible. For many families, institutional care for a sick child is no longer inevitable. Instead, the extent of the damage—if there is any—need not prevent the child from leading a happy, useful life in society.

Who Are The Patients?

Over 7 percent (232,000 annually) of American newborns weigh 5-1/2 pounds (2500 grams) or less. Babies weighing 4 lbs. 6 oz. (2000 grams) or less are particularly susceptible to critical illness. These dangerously small infants often have problems with breathing, heart action, and control of temperature and blood sugar. Unless these difficulties can be controlled, they may lead to brain damage or death. Many of the infants in an ICN are babies with other birth defects such as open spine, intestinal or stomach defects, and heart defects.

Some of the tiny patients in an ICN are recovering from surgery. Remarkable advances in pediatric surgery are saving many thousands of babies who previously faced almost certain death. Ingenious surgical techniques have been developed for correcting congenital heart, stomach, and intestinal defects and for helping babies born with open spine (spina bifida) and water on the brain (hydrocephalus).

Causes Of Low Birthweight

Five-and-a-half pounds (2500 grams) is generally considered the dividing line between normal and low birthweight. Low-birthweight infants are the result of true prematurity or impaired fetal growth. A premature infant has been expelled from the womb before his organs have fully matured. Reasons for true prematurity are not usually understood, but the most commonly recognized causes are early rupture of the membranes, multiple pregnancies, bleeding problems during pregnancy, and maternal infections.

Impaired fetal growth results in a ''small for date'' baby, who is born at term but has low birthweight. Poor maternal nutrition, before and during pregnancy, is often associated with poor fetal growth. These infants suffer *in utero* from poor nutrition, poor oxygenation, and other adverse conditions. Contributing factors are poverty; congenital defects; race (nonwhites have a higher incidence of low birthweight than whites, which is perhaps a reflection of poverty and poor nutrition); excessive smoking; and age of the mother (the highest incidence is in mothers under twenty).

Who Staffs The Nursery?

The people who run an intensive care nursery make up the crucial element in its success. There are more physicians and nurses than patients here because high-risk infants demand full-time attention. These highly trained, dedicated men and women are specialists in the challenging field of neonatal care. Neonatal refers to the first four weeks after birth. The entire span of pregnancy through the first four weeks after birth is called the perinatal period. More lives are lost and more permanent disabilities are incurred during this period than at any other time in life.

Neonatal nurse-clinicians are key figures in the ICN. They are a new breed of "supernurses" who assume responsibilities in some areas traditionally reserved for physicians. They are the only staff members who are constantly in the ICN, so they are in the best position to spot problems as soon as things go wrong and provide support for families. Of course, physicians are constantly on call in the ICN; trained hospital residents are immediately responsible for day and night duty.

Saving a sick newborn may mean immediate treatment for respiratory distress, cardiac failure, or convulsions. The nurse-clinician must be knowledgeable about the techniques to be used and skilled at using them, even with the sickest, smallest infants. In an emergency, such decisions cannot await a physician's arrival, with death or irreversible damage imminent.

The March of Dimes Birth Defects Foundation supports this expanded role for nurses. There is a dearth of highly qualified nurses, especially in the area of maternal and child care. To increase the number of nurses able to provide intensive care for high-risk mothers and infants, the voluntary health organization has made grants to educate nurse-clinicians at a growing number of university teaching hospitals around the country.

To qualify as neonatal nurse-clinicians, they must be registered nurses, who have completed postgraduate education in high-risk maternal-fetal care. The educational program includes clinical and classroom experience. Perinatal and neonatal care is interdisciplinary; nurse-clinicians and physicians work together.

Helping Parents Cope In A Crisis

Neonatal nurse-clinicians use the newest, most sophisticated equipment in caring for high-risk newborns, but handling machinery is only part of the job. They also help parents cope with the crisis of having a high-risk infant. They are called upon to comfort and teach parents who find it difficult to cope with the shock of learning that their baby needs intensive care.

The Intensive Care Nursery, Part 2

by Dr. Ralph W. Gause

When a baby is born too soon or too small, he is usually at risk because his immature body cannot function normally. His life may be threatened by breathing difficulties, erratic heart action, temperature fluctuations, and poor regulation of body chemistry.

Technical achievements now make it possible to alleviate many of these problems in the intensive care nursery (ICN). Here the baby lives in his own environment, often an Isolette incubator. From the moment of his arrival until he is ready to go home, everything about him—the way he breathes, his temperature, his heartbeat and blood pressure, his blood-sugar level, his nervous system—is monitored by a formidable array of equipment. Much as a home smoke alarm detects small amounts of smoke, alarms sound if minor changes in the baby's heart and breathing rates occur. As part of its concern to protect the unborn and the newborn, the March of Dimes Birth Defects Foundation has provided funds for many intensive care nurseries across the nation. The voluntary health organization has also given aid to smaller hospitals for safe, swift transportation of critically ill newborns to intensive care nurseries in larger hospitals.

Respiratory Distress Syndrome

The most common and yet most serious problem of infants at risk is respiratory distress syndrome (RDS), also known as hyaline membrane disease. It is a perplexing and critical illness in premature babies. Though the death rate has been reduced considerably in recent years, about one out of six babies afflicted with the malady—a combination of immature development and inadequate physiological maturity—dies every year.

Among the methods used to save babies with breathing difficulties, including respiratory distress syndrome, is a technique known as continuous positive airway pressure. By inserting a tube in the baby's windpipe or placing a pressurized hood around his head, a continuous supply of oxygen under low pressure is directed to the infant's lungs to prevent them from collapsing.

In the past it was difficult to determine the exact amount of oxygen required by an immature baby. Too much or too little oxygen may produce serious complications. Not enough may lead to brain damage or death. Too much can cause blindness or permanent lung damage. Blood gas monitors in the ICN eliminate the guesswork. Skin sensors are being developed to report continually on the level of oxygen and other gases in the baby's blood.

Other Problems For Babies At Risk

Underweight newborns often have trouble controlling body temperature because their central nervous system is immature, and they don't have enough body fat to prevent the loss of body heat. They also are unable to shiver and sweat, which are effective temperature regulators. Incubators have long been used to keep premature babies warm. Some babies require extra warmth in the incubator and are placed on a warm water mattress called an Aqua-pad. Or they may have a small plastic dome, called a heat shield, placed over their bodies to prevent further heat loss. In many ICNs today, babies who are severely ill and have a number of tubes and wires attached to them are cared for while lying on an open table. Unlike the old-style incubator that took half an hour to heat, the table's overhead radiant warmer heats instantly. The temperature is controlled automatically by sensors attached to the infant's skin. Open sides on the table allow the baby to be x-rayed, fed, changed, operated on, and cuddled while he is still under the radiant heat. The nursery staff is also able to observe the infant more easily.

Jaundice in some degree is not unusual in normal newborns, but it is often exaggerated in premature babies and in infants with Rh blood incompatibility. This means that the liver is too immature to detoxify the waste product, bilirubin. Severe jaundice, also called hyperbilirubinemia, if untreated, could lead to brain damage or death. Accumulated bilirubin can be partially or totally broken down into harmless substances, however, by exposing the naked infant to a bright fluorescent light over a period of hours. In the most severe cases of hyperbilirubinemia, the infant requires replacement of his blood—an exchange transfusion.

Feeding immature newborns was once a serious problem. Some babies had to wait several days to be fed because their underdeveloped digestive systems were unable to tolerate sufficient amounts of food. Even after feeding began, it was laborious. Only tiny amounts of formula could be absorbed by the baby at one time.

Another problem arises because these babies need more nutrients than mature newborns but often have trouble swallowing and sucking.

Now infusion pumps deliver fluids to the baby's bloodstream at the needed rate through a tiny tube inserted in the umbilical artery. This technique, called total parenteral nutrition, saves many infants who would previously have died of prolonged inability to take in food normally. Solutions with a mixture of calories, protein, minerals, trace elements, and vitamins are fed drop by drop into the baby's bloodstream until he gains weight and can begin or resume oral feeding.

Every Hospital Doesn't Have An ICN

Not every hospital can afford an intensive care nursery. Nor does every hospital need one. Expensive equipment and the extremely high cost of maintaining specially trained staff to attend the nursery full-time, would be economically wasteful for a small hospital. Perinatologists agree that regional hospital care is the best answer to newborn intensive care.

In a major effort to solve the problem, the March of Dimes has published the report of the Committee on Perinatal Health: "Toward Improving the Outcome of Pregnancy." It outlines a plan for making health personnel, skills, and facilities available to the largest number of people without costly duplication.

The March of Dimes helped organize the Committee, which was made up of representatives from the American Academy of Family Physicians, the American Academy of Pediatrics, the American College of Obstetricians and Gynecologists, and the American Medical Association.

One of the Committee's key recommendations was that regional medical care for high-risk babies be divided among three types of hospitals. Fully equipped intensive care nurseries would be available in the largest hospitals. In a densely populated urban area, there may be several hospitals with ICNs. In less populated areas, a single perinatal center could serve several community hospitals. Medium-sized hospitals would be equipped to care for all but the sickest infants. All small local hospitals would be equipped for emergency transportation of infants at risk to the larger center.

Critically ill babies born in a hospital without an ICN can be taken to a perinatal center by ambulance, airplane, or helicopter. In these emergency situations physicians can use a "perinatal hotline" by telephoning experts at the center before sending their patients to the nearest ICN. During the trip the infant rides in a special transport Isolette and is attended by nurses or physicians. Medical care can begin at once if necessary because the transport vehicle, whether it travels by land or air, carries life-support and monitoring equipment.

Of course, the best way to transport a baby who has been predicted as high-risk is to transfer the pregnant mother to a hospital with an intensive care nursery prior to the birth of the infant.

Miracles can and do happen every day in an intensive care nursery. Physicians and nurses there have a remarkable arsenal of tools, drugs, and techniques to save their tiny patients. When this very special combination of expertise and equipment is available to every immature and sick infant in the United States, we will see a new generation of healthier, stronger babies.

Glossary Of ICN Medical Terms

Some intensive care nurseries prepare special brochures to help parents better understand the care their babies are receiving. The Turner Neonatal Intensive Care Unit of Hermann Hospital in Houston, Texas, has published an especially clear and reassuring booklet, ''They Need Love To Grow,'' which includes a detailed description of the unit and how it works. The March of Dimes assisted in its publication. Following are extracts from the brochure's glossary of medical terms.

Apnea—Lack of breathing.

Bilirubin lights—Special fluorescent light bulbs used in phototherapy to help the baby's blood break down the potentially harmful bilirubin particles in the blood; done by placing the lights over the baby after covering his eyes and removing his clothing.

Bilirubin—A normal product in the bloodstream that comes from the red blood cells and can cause a yellowish coloring of the skin if the level is high.

Blood chemistries—Measurements of various substances in the blood, such as sodium, chloride, potassium, sugar, and bilirubin.

Blood gases—Blood tests done to determine the pH (acid-base balance) and concentration of oxygen and carbon dioxide in the blood. They estimate how well the heart and lungs are functioning.

Bradycardia—Very slow heart rate.

CPAP (Continuous Positive Airway Pressure)—A method of keeping a certain amount of pressure in the baby's lungs to help them remain open or fully expanded.

Cyanosis; duskiness—Bluish color of the skin caused by poor circulation or low oxygen concentration in the bloodstream.

Distended abdomen—Full, tight appearance of baby's stomach (abdomen).

EEG: Electroencephalogram—Test to measure the brain wave pattern.

EKG; ECG; Electrocardiogram—Test done to measure the heartbeat pattern.

Electrolytes—One of a set of blood chemistries that includes the sodium, potassium, and chloride concentrations in the blood.

Exchange transfusion—Procedure done to rid the baby's bloodstream of harmful products, whereby the baby's blood is replaced with donor blood, exchanging a small amount at a time.

Gavage feedings—A method of feeding the baby fluids by inserting a small plastic tube through the mouth or nose into the stomach.

Gestational age—Age of a baby in weeks from the time he was conceived to the time of birth. The gestational age for a full-term baby is 38-42 weeks. A preterm baby is one born at less than 38 weeks, and a post-term baby is one born after 42 weeks gestation. Babies are classified in one of nine categories according to their gestational age and their birthweight.

Heat shield—A small plastic dome placed over the baby's body to decrease heat loss.

Heel stick—A small prick in the baby's heel in order to obtain blood for testing; similar to finger stick in adults.

Hyperalimentation fluid—A solution of sugar water (glucose), protein (amino acids), and sometimes fat (lipids), plus added vitamins, that is given intravenously to help the baby grow and gain weight; usually given when we cannot totally feed the baby formula by mouth; also called IVH or HAF.

Intubate—Placing a small plastic tube into the baby's trachea (windpipe) to assist the baby's breathing.

ISC; Servo-control—A method of keeping a baby warm in an incubator, whereby the incubator temperature is regulated by the baby's own skin temperature.

Isolation—Restriction of baby to incubator when an infection is suspected; it requires extra hand-washing and often special disposal of linens and diapers.

Incubator; Isolette—Heated, completely enclosed bed.

Monitor—A machine that allows us to know at all times the baby's heart rate or breathing rate. To use a monitor, we tape electrodes to the baby's chest, arms, or legs, that transmit the heart rate or breathing rate to the monitor.

Oxygen analyzer—An instrument placed inside the oxygen hood to allow the doctors and nurses to know the amount of concentration of oxygen the baby is receiving at all times.

Oxygen hood—A small plastic, dome-shaped hood that is placed over a baby's head to provide him with the proper amount of oxygen he needs.

Respirator; ventilator—A machine used to breathe for a baby.

Retractions—A "caved-in" appearance of the chest as the baby breathes.

Sepsis; septic—A term used to describe an internal infection.

Suction catheter—A small plastic tube inserted in the nose, mouth, or tracheal tube to remove mucus.

Tachypnea—Very fast breathing rate.

Transport incubator—A special incubator on wheels, with its own oxygen supply and heater; used to transfer babies from outside hospitals and to and from the operating room and x-ray department within the hospital.

UA catheter; Umbilical artery catheter—A plastic tube inserted into the artery in the baby's umbilicus (navel); used to give the baby glucose water infusions, medications, and to withdraw blood to check different blood chemistries.

A Pediatrician Discusses Immunizations
by Dr. Alvin N. Eden

Bacteria have existed since time began. Whole populations were wiped out by epidemics before the study of immunology gave us vaccines to protect against these terrible diseases. The vaccines currently available are safe, easy to administer, and effective. Despite this, a large percentage of our children are still inadequately protected. In this day and age it is criminal not to see to it that each and every child is immunized against the diseases for which we have protective vaccines.

The main purpose of this article is to remind all of you to get busy right now! You must make sure that your child receives all the immunizations he requires. This means that he should be fully protected by the time he is two years old. There is no excuse for neglecting this important area of health care.

Many of us still vividly remember the dreaded fear of smallpox and the horror of living through a polio epidemic. Nowadays, hardly anybody gives these killer diseases a second thought. In 1980 a needle in the arm or rump, or a few drops of a sugary liquid into the mouth, and presto—permanent protection against another vicious disease. With the widespread use of these vaccines, the incidence of these illnesses has decreased tremendously. As a result, too many of us have been lulled into a false sense of security. These dangerous and potentially lethal bugs are still around. If enough children are not given their immunizations, the chance of an epidemic increases. The sad fact is that over five million preschool children are currently not fully immunized and protected. One out of three preschoolers is inadequately protected against one or more diseases. This is a disgraceful situation and must be corrected.

Q. What is immunization?

A. An immunization is a safe and effective method that protects the body against certain diseases. The material that is given by injection or by mouth stimulates the body to produce substances called antibodies. The function of these antibodies is to fight off that particular disease whenever it attempts to invade the body. The protection that these antibodies produce is called immunity. After receiving the proper immunization, the child becomes immune to (protected against) the disease for many years and often for life.

Q. What diseases should my child be immunized against?

A. Every child should be routinely immunized against the following seven diseases: polio, diphtheria, tetanus, pertussis (whooping cough), measles, rubella (German measles), and mumps. The child should be fully immunized by the time he is two years old.

Q. Why not wait until the child is ready to start school before immunizing him?

A. Unfortunately, this is what happens in many cases. Children are unprotected during their first four or five years of life, and this is just the time when they are most vulnerable to many of these illnesses. If an epidemic were ever to occur, they would be in very serious trouble. So it makes no sense to wait.

Q. Why should we worry about the unimmunized child? Isn't it true that their chances of getting infected by one of these diseases are very small?

A. The answer is very simple. It is true that the incidence of these diseases is now low. But a very dangerous situation is developing. First of all, this approach is causing more and more children to remain unimmunized and unprotected. This increases the risk of an epidemic. As a matter of fact, there have been small outbreaks of measles in recent years in areas where a large percentage of the children were not immunized against measles. And there is a second danger developing. There now is a reduced opportunity for unimmunized children to acquire immunity by a mild or asymptomatic natural infection. It therefore follows that these children are likely to grow up unprotected, and when they become adults and have their own children, their infants are at great risk. The mothers can't transfer any immunity to their newborns. The effects of many of these diseases are most serious during the first few months of life, when the central nervous system (brain) is most vulnerable. Let's take measles as an example. If the pregnant woman has not had the measles vaccination or the natural disease, she will not transmit any immunity to her unborn baby during the pregnancy, and the baby will be born unprotected against measles for the first six months of life. An infant who gets measles can become seriously ill and may even die from it. The mother who has had the measles vaccine or the disease itself will naturally protect her new baby—and this protection lasts about six months. At age fifteen months, a baby should receive immunization for measles to assure lifelong protection. (A child between the ages of six and fifteen months who has not yet been immunized is vulnerable to measles and should be immunized immediately if a measles epidemic occurs in your community. He will then need to be re-immunized at the regular time.)

Q. *What segments of the population are not being adequately immunized?*

A. All segments are involved. Although the problem is greatest in the inner cities and urban ghettos and among the rural poor, many thousands of middle class children are also inadequately protected. A recent study reported in a pediatric journal clearly illustrated the scope of the problem. In checking over the records of a group of Idaho private pediatricians, it was found that less than 40 percent of their regular patients were completely immunized by two years of age. Children taken to clinics had an even poorer record—only 22 percent were fully immunized.

Q. *At what age should my new baby start to be immunized?*

A. Most pediatricians start their immunization routine when the baby is two months of age.

Q. *Is there a recommended schedule for active immunization of infants?*

A. Yes, there is. The schedule suggested by the American Academy of Pediatrics is the one followed by many physicians. There is room to deviate from this schedule, and many doctors work out a routine that they find most efficient and effective for their purposes. The following is the Academy's immunization schedule:

Age:	*Immunization:*
Two Months	DPT*, Trivalent Oral Polio
Four Months	DPT, Trivalent Oral Polio
Six Months	DPT
Twelve Months	Tuberculin Test
Fifteen Months	M.M.R.**
Eighteen Months	DPT, Trivalent Oral Polio
Four to Six Years	DPT, Trivalent Oral Polio

*DPT—Diphtheria, Pertussis, Tetanus

**M.M.R.—Measles, Mumps, Rubella

The measles, mumps, and rubella vaccines may also be given separately. If given when the child is fifteen months of age or older, permanent, lifelong protection results, and no boosters are needed.

Q. What about smallpox vaccination?

A. Routine smallpox vaccination is no longer recommended. The last case of smallpox in the United States was in 1949. According to the latest word from the World Health Organization, smallpox has been completely eradicated all over the world. The last few cases were reported in Africa and India.

There is a greater risk from the possible complications of the smallpox vaccine than from the disease. Therefore, both the U.S. Public Health Service and the American Academy of Pediatrics recommend that smallpox vaccination no longer be given.

Q. Why bother vaccinating against measles, mumps, and rubella? Aren't these "simple" childhood diseases and not dangerous ones?

A. Absolutely not. Serious and even fatal complications can occur after any of these "simple" diseases. For example, encephalitis (inflammation of the brain) may follow both measles and mumps and can cause permanent brain damage. If a pregnant woman gets rubella during the first three months of her pregnancy, there is a strong possibility that her newborn will be born with serious congenital malformations. It is just as important to immunize your child against measles, mumps, and rubella as it is to protect him against polio, diphtheria, and tetanus.

Q. What about tetanus boosters after cuts or wounds?

A. If the child is fully immunized, meaning that he has received three DPT shots followed by a fourth, one year after the third, no boosters are needed for at least five years—even if he gets a puncture wound from a rusty nail. After the tetanus booster is given, around the time the child starts school, additional boosters should be given every ten years. If a child suffers a possibly contaminated wound and has not had a tetanus booster during the previous five years, a booster is required.

Q. What is the tuberculin test?

A. This is a screening skin test to determine if the child was ever exposed to tuberculosis. It is not an immunization against tuberculosis. The test is repeated at varying intervals, depending on the risk of exposure and the prevalence of tuberculosis in that population group.

Q. What reactions can we expect after the various immunizations?

A. The following:

1) Polio: None

2) DPT: Occasionally some fever and/or crankiness, which starts a few hours after the injection and may last a day or so. In rare instances, this fever can be quite high, and in such cases the baby's doctor should be notified. There also may be some redness and swelling at the site of the needle, which disappear in short order.

3) M.M.R.: In some cases, fever develops between five to twelve days after the injection. At times, a rash also appears at the time of the fever. This reaction may last a day or two and is no cause for concern.

This completes what I want to tell you about immunizations. I hope that my message has gotten through. It is your responsibility to see to it that your child is fully immunized by as early an age as possible. The stakes are high, and there is no time to waste.

Hypothyroid Screening
by Jean Caldwell

A simple test can save 1,000 babies from mental retardation. Is your state using it?

Friends call Rebecca Weatherbee "a miracle baby."

At three she is a bright, healthy little girl—able to speak in both Spanish and English, ride a two-wheeler (with training wheels), and keep her mother, Carol, father, Roy, and big brother, Jeff, on their toes by getting into everything.

If she had been born a few years earlier, she would have been severely retarded.

Carol Weatherbee remembers how she felt when she got the phone call that changed Becky's life.

"I panicked—absolutely panicked."

The call came from Magee Women's Hospital in Pittsburgh, where Becky had been born ten days earlier. Someone was explaining that Dr. Thomas Foley was running a pilot program testing for hypothyroidism. Becky's thyroid level was "very, very low. We don't know if it's cretinism; your pediatrician will call you."

Carol Weatherbee had a vision of "something grotesque—something that you didn't want for anyone."

Cretinism, which results from hypothyroidism or low thyroid levels in infants, is a tragic condition in which severe mental retardation accompanies stunted growth.

Although few parents have ever heard of hypothyroidism, it affects an average of one baby in 4,000—making it four times more prevalent than phenylketonouria (PKU), a metabolic disorder which also causes mental retardation and for which 40 states have enacted mandatory screening laws.

A baby may appear normal at birth despite being born with a deficient thyroid gland. By the time the signs of hypothyroidism can be seen on clinical examination, irreversible brain damage will have occurred.

Rebecca Weatherbee is a bright, normal little girl today because of a technological breakthrough that made a screening test possible. By identifying her condition soon after she was born, doctors were able to begin treatment with the vital thyroid hormone when she was only two weeks old.

What Happens Without Treatment

Consider the case of a Canadian family. They live in the province of Quebec, which started the world's first mass screening program of newborns for hypothyroidism. They are a well-educated, high-income family. They received the message: bring your baby in for further examination, tests, and treatment.

Their reply in effect: nonsense! Our baby is perfectly well, and we are not going to be bothered with a lot of tests.

About a year later word came through to the screening room that a doctor in a university clinic specializing in child development had found a year-old child who was a true cretin: severely retarded, dwarfed, large and protruding tongue, arms and legs too short for the size of the trunk, coarse features in an unusual-looking face, and suffering from digestive problems.

Had the province-wide screening test failed to spot this unfortunate child? A check of files revealed the story: clipped to the card indicating that the test had indeed identified this infant as hypothyroid was the letter from the parents saying they could see no reason for testing a baby who was perfectly well.

Physicians have been trained to spot abnormalities in newborns, and they have a great deal of experience in examining babies. How easy is it for a doctor to tell if a child is hypothyroid without a test?

Ann Bennett, regional coordinator for the New England Hypothyroid Screening Program located in the State Institute of Laboratories in Boston, relates this story:

Two babies with the same last name were born on the same day in the same hospital and cared for by the same doctor. Both were screened for hypothyroidism. One test was positive.

Following her usual procedure, Bennett phoned the baby's doctor and said that the baby (whom we will call Baby Robinson) was hypothyroid.

"I'm not surprised," the physician replied. "That little girl has several problems." And he reeled them off.

"No, no!" exclaimed Bennett. "I'm not talking about a girl. I'm talking about Baby Boy Robinson."

"The boy?" echoed the startled doctor. "The boy is perfect. There's nothing wrong with the boy. The blood samples must have gotten mixed up.''

A hasty recheck of both babies confirmed the original findings. The girl, for all her other problems, had no trouble with her thyroid function. The ''perfect'' boy, on the other hand, could have become retarded if his condition had not been caught through a bit of dried blood on a piece of filter paper one-eighth inch in diameter.

The Importance of Screening

Dr. Reed Larsen, head of the thyroid unit at Peter Bent Brigham Hospital in Boston, who does the confirmatory testing for the screening program, emphasizes the importance of screening by noting that of the first 227 babies found to be hypothyroid in three regional and two municipal screening programs, only eight babies had any symptoms.

The test to screen infants for hypothyroidism has the potential of saving over 1,000 babies a year in the United States from mental retardation. (This figure is based on an incidence of one hypothyroid baby in every 4,000 born and the slightly more than four million births reported in 1977 in the U.S., Puerto Rico, Guam, the Virgin Islands, and the District of Columbia.) Yet some states are dragging their feet on instituting the test, and parents are being urged to see that screening gets started in their localities.

Thyroid hormone is essential to normal growth, especially during the first five months of life when the brain cells grow most rapidly.

A baby without enough thyroid hormone during these crucial early months suffers irreversible brain damage. Some researchers believe that retardation is inevitable if treatment is not begun before the child is three months old.

As far back as the early 1800s, medical authorities had linked the lack of thyroid function to cretinism. They have known for years that oral administration of thyroid hormone can improve the physical health of hypothyroid patients— although it can never undo early brain damage.

What was lacking was a mass screening test to pick out the one baby in 4,000 who is hypothyroid before the visible signs appear. The breakthrough came from research being done by doctors whose special interest was neither newborns nor thyroid glands.

Dr. Rosalyn Yalow and the late Dr. Solomon Berson were interested in monitoring insulin metabolism in diabetics. Aided by funds from the National Institute of Health, they invented a procedure called radioimmunoassay.

This made it possible to measure many substances from a tiny spot of dried blood on a piece of filter paper. Dr. Yalow received the Nobel Prize in medicine for her work.

Dr. Jean Dussault learned about radioimmunoassay in California, where he was doing research on the thyroid gland and its importance in fetal development.

When he returned to Quebec, he began working in a laboratory "five feet away" from the laboratory that held blood samples from every newborn in the province. In Canada, as in the United States since the mid-1960s, about 90 percent of all babies routinely have their heels pricked for a miniscule blood sample before they leave the hospital. This dried blood is then tested for PKU. There is ample blood left on the filter paper after the PKU test to perform other tests.

"When I saw those spots," Dr. Dussault remembers, "I thought that I would try to devise a test for hypothyroidism."

He succeeded.

That was in the fall of 1972. In April 1974, a screening program for hypothyroidism was set up for the entire province with Dr. Dussault in charge. From then through August 1978, 383,000 babies were screened and 97 were identified as being hypothyroid.

As each baby is identified, he undergoes a series of confirmatory tests and then is put on a simple and inexpensive program of therapy. All the mother must do is mash up a small pill, which costs pennies a day, and give it to the baby daily with some food. The babies are being followed to keep careful check on their physical and mental growth, and all are doing well.

Testing Throughout The World

Word of the breakthrough spread through professional journals. Doctors in Japan, Belgium, Austria, and Australia began to plan for screening programs in their countries.

By 1979, 36 centers in 12 European countries including Denmark, Finland, Germany, Italy, the Netherlands, Spain, Sweden, Switzerland and the United Kingdom were screening for hypothyroidism. After half a million newborns were screened, doctors reported that they were finding one out of every 3,800 babies suffered from hypothyroidism. An article published by the Newborn Committee of the European Thyroid Association says this "unexpected frequency" is "a powerful argument for obtaining from European governments the recognition, recommendation, and financing for systematic screening programs."

In May 1975, Dr. William Murphey, director of the Oregon State Public Health Laboratory, added hypothyroid testing to the regional neonatal screening program, which now includes the states of Alaska, Montana, Idaho, and Nevada, as well as Oregon.

In January 1976, Massachusetts set up a screening program that quickly expanded to test blood samples from babies born in Connecticut, Rhode Island, Maine, and New Hampshire. As in Oregon, this New England program also screens for rarer metabolic diseases such as galactosemia and maple sugar urine disease.

Vermont, Maryland, Michigan, and Utah also started to screen infants for hypothyroidism.

But the bandwagon effect may be only an illusion. Gatlin Brandon, retired director of the State Health Department Laboratory in Oregon, told the 59th Conference of Public Health Lab Directors recently that six state public health laboratories did not report any metabolic screening tests for the fiscal year 1978 and that ten state labs have programs for PKU testing only. Some states, including some with more than 100,000 births yearly, have mandated hypothyroid screening but are not doing it because no money has been appropriated.

Brandon's goal is the establishment of 32 regional screening laboratories in the U.S. All newborns could then be tested for hypothyroidism, PKU, and several rarer metabolic disorders.

What Parents Can Do

The National Association for Retarded Citizens (NARC) has long urged parents to push for neonatal screening in their own states.

Parents can ask their own doctor if their new baby will be screened. They can call state health officials to ask why not if the answer is no. They can spread word of the availability of the test by writing to newspapers and magazines, and they can join their local Association for Retarded Citizens to exert political pressure to institute screening.

Dr. Robert Guthrie of Buffalo, N.Y., the originator of the widely used test for PKU and himself the parent of a retarded child, admits that new knowledge and new ideas spread slowly. "But when it's something important that will prevent lifelong retardation in a baby, you like to speed it up. More and more parents need to raise hell with medical centers, states, and Congress to get on with this. Parents have to push for regionalization... talk to politicians... and push to get specimens collected across state lines."

Despite the success of the program in Massachusetts, it almost came to a screeching halt in the summer of 1977. The State Institute of Laboratories had started hypothyroid screening as a pilot study with federal funds. When the federal grant expired, the Department of Public Health put in a routine budget request for $63,000 for the salaries of the technicians assigned to the program. But the legislature was feeling an economic crunch. The House of Representatives decided to eliminate all new state positions and lopped the money from the budget.

There was an instant uproar.

Some states and some Canadian provinces are hampered in starting the tests because the blood samples for PKU do not go to one central laboratory but rather to a number of private laboratories.

Other states have budget difficulties. Dr. Edwin Naylor, research assistant professor in the Department of Pediatrics of the State University of New York at Buffalo Medical School, warns that unless legislatures appropriate funds when they mandate screening programs, "It could drag on for years and never be done."

Dr. Naylor speculates that the day may come when officials in a state that does not do hypothyroid screening could be hauled into court by the parents of a hypothyroid child who will charge: "You knew about screening years ago but you did nothing. Now our child is retarded and we want you to pay."

Already mothers are comparing notes. In Boston Dr. Marvin Mitchell, who heads the New England Regional Screening Program, tells this story: two mothers sat in a physician's waiting room. One held a baby only three weeks old.

"I'm scared," she confided. "The doctor told me to bring my baby right in because he is hypothyroid. I don't know what that means."

The second woman looked up at the tiny baby and said, "It means you're lucky. My son is hypothyroid, too, but they didn't find out in time and now he is retarded."

If your state does not screen newborns for hypothyroidism, your pediatrician should be able to have a hospital or private laboratory do the test. The cost would probably be around $10—much higher on an individual basis than when mass screening is done.

The Basics Of Bottle-Feeding
by Marie Simon, R.N.

There's a lot more to bottle-feeding than putting a nipple in baby's mouth and burping him at regular intervals.

The resurgence of breast-feeding as the popular method of infant feeding has been largely due to the public's greater interest and education in nutrition. There is a major trend toward breast-feeding; nonetheless, there are still vast numbers of women bottle-feeding their babies. These mothers and their babies are perhaps being deprived of the education and support so vital for a satisfying experience, simply because of great interest in breast-feeding. If you have decided to bottle-feed your baby, perhaps the following information will assist you in making the most of it.

Establishing Trust

Before any techniques of infant feeding can be discussed, it is necessary to understand the little person you are feeding. Every baby is an individual, and as a new parent, you will soon see that your baby differs from other babies in such things as height, weight, hair growth, tooth eruption, talking, walking and disposition. When discussing infants, you must keep this in mind, for although statements made are applicable to *most* babies, they may not always pertain to *your* baby.

During the first day of life, an infant will already show his preferences and dislikes. It has often been thought that in addition to other physiological reasons, an infant cries at birth because he has had to leave the embracing, warm womb and enter into a cold world where lights shine brightly and there is much commotion. Despite nature's built-in mechanisms for survival, the infant has yet to develop trust in anyone and may be signaling to us that he is not sure he will be fed or cared for or loved. Establishing a trust with your infant is an ongoing process that should be part of the feeding procedure.

Cuddling is one way to make an infant feel secure. Holding an infant close while feeding will not only make him feel safe, but will also let him know who is caring for him. Infants have a keen sense of smell and hearing and can differentiate mother from father simply by their individual odors and voices.

Infants can see best at a distance of about twelve inches, so hold your baby during a feeding so that he can see you, smell you, and cuddle close to you. To help get the formula into his stomach, he should be in a position somewhere

between sitting and lying. This will prevent milk from pooling at the back of the throat where it can cause choking. If choking should occur, it will be easier to change the infant's position quickly if he is partially upright.

Be sure to talk to your infant while feeding him. Then he will quickly get to know and trust you. And make sure that he is comfortable: pillows and chairs with arms are very helpful.

Reflexes Are Important

You may think all there is to bottle-feeding is putting the nipple into your baby's mouth and burping him at regular intervals. But did you know that babies have reflexes that can affect the feeding process? These reflexes include rooting, tongue protrusion, sucking, and grasping. Knowing about them is just one more way to understand your infant.

Rooting Reflex: This reflex is elicited by stroking one side of the infant's face near his mouth or chin. He will then turn toward the side stroked. When feeding, there is no need to push the baby's head toward the bottle; simply stroke the side of his face where you want to feed him.

Tongue Protrusion Reflex: This reflex is best seen when an infant is offered solid foods because the tongue sticks out when stimulated. It is especially apparent during the first three months of life and can be mistaken for a dislike of an offered food. To ensure that the infant is getting more food into his mouth than on his chin or bib, put the food farther back on his tongue. (Be sure not to gag your baby by putting the spoon too far back.) Unless he desires more than his required amount of formula, you can take the reflex as a hint that solids need not be introduced yet. In fact, many physicians now recommend delaying the introduction of solid foods until the baby is four to six months old.

The Sucking Reflex: Because this reflex is present *in utero,* an infant can already have a sucking callous on the middle of his upper lip when he is born. The newborn will attempt to suck on anything put into his mouth, and as any breast-feeding mother will tell you, the suck is very strong. The need to suck is as important as the need to eat, so ample time must be given to this during feedings. Keep in mind, however, that the need to suck is separate from the desire for food, so intense sucking does not always imply hunger. To meet his sucking needs, the baby may suck his fingers or sleeve even after being fed. Some parents prefer that their baby suck on a pacifier instead.

If you wish to have your infant fulfill his sucking needs with a pacifier, keep in mind that any pacifier you can pull apart, an infant may be able to pull apart. To be safe, purchase pacifiers that come in only one or two pieces, without small pieces that can become dislodged and choke the baby. Pacifiers that are sterilized will need to be replaced from time to time, just as bottle nipples will. This is because heat causes rubber to stretch, and it can snap apart more easily.

The Grasping Reflex: When an infant clasps an object that comes in contact with his palms, he exhibits this reflex. It is so strong that you could pull an infant off a table simply by putting a finger in each hand. Parents with long hair and necklaces should be aware of this when in contact with the infant, and not just during feedings.

Feeding Problems

A formula suitable for one baby may cause gas, spitting-up, vomiting, constipation, diarrhea or allergy in another. For this reason it is very important that you keep your doctor or nurse practitioner informed of any side effects from a particular formula. It is unwise to change from one formula to another without medical advice—especially because often it is not the formula that is causing the problems.

Spitting-up is a common behavior of newborns. It is different from vomiting in that it is equal to or less than the amount consumed. To help relieve your baby of this annoying occurrence, try the following:

Don't let your infant indulge in excessive crying before feedings. This means feeding your infant when he is hungry. Be sure any schedule is designed with the infant's hunger times in mind and not just with your schedule, although that is important to consider too. Feed him on a fairly regular basis, usually no sooner than three hours from the last feeding. (There is also the belief that feeding on demand is best. If you decide that this is best for your baby, feeding times will be different.)

If the baby seems to want to eat more often, consider whether he is merely wanting to suck (try a pacifier); is not necessarily hungry but perhaps thirsty (try plain warm tap water supplements); is wet (may need diapering); hurts (fever? irritability? listlessness?); or is bored (try cuddling, talking, and playing with him). In any event, excessive crying means large intakes of air into the stomach, and if formula is fed on top of this air, it will soon be spit out when the infant burps.

Avoid introducing air into your baby during feedings. This is not always easy because some infants "gulp" their milk. Check the nipple holes to be sure milk is coming out in drops, not in a steady stream. Remember, old nipples and those continually boiled will often have larger holes. If more milk is coming into baby's mouth than he is sucking for, he will find it difficult to keep pace and will increase his swallowing—thus gulping down his milk.

Don't let your baby suck on an empty or nearly empty bottle, where air can easily be sucked in. To discourage this, always make sure the nipple is full of milk. One way to do so is to fill the bottle with a little more milk than you expect the baby to take (and be prepared to discard the extra amount). The best way to make sure your infant does not take in air is to feed him yourself; never prop the bottle.

Give the baby time to drink. Babies are nose breathers, and the increased activity of feeding increases the need to breathe faster. To compensate, a baby will often suck for a few minutes, stop and rest, and then suck again. During these rest periods, do not jiggle the bottle in the baby's mouth. He will resume eating when ready. Also make sure that the baby's nose is not obstructed with the bottle nipple, impairing his breathing. If the infant keeps falling asleep, try uncovering him before feeding.

Burp your infant at intervals. This can be done in several ways The infant can be placed in a sitting position on your lap (be sure to support his head and back) or on your shoulder. Then either rub his back with upward strokes or gently pat it. Sometimes just the change in position will dislodge air without any patting or rubbing. Frequent burping helps to get air out, which discourages spitting-up and gas pains.

Overfeeding can lead to spitting-up and vomiting. Bottle-fed babies tend to be overfed more often than breast-fed babies, probably because one is apt to gauge the baby's food needs by what is left in the bottle rather than by the baby's actions.

Vomiting may occur after the introduction of solids. The stomach capacity of newborns averages approximately two ounces. Since today's iron formulas contain all the nutrients needed for the first six months of life, introducing solids early (with the resultant vomiting or increased spitting-up in some babies) is foolish. Again, check with your pediatrician. And avoid engaging the baby in vigorous activity or play directly after eating.

Constipation can result from feeding as well as from other causes. Turning red in the face, pulling up the legs, screaming and grunting while having a bowel movement, do not signify constipation in themselves, but dry, hard, pellet-like stools do. Bottle-fed babies will occasionally experience constipation, but as long as it is not an everyday experience and the baby is otherwise well, you need not be concerned. Simply adding more water to baby's diet, or water with a little bit of sugar in it, will help the infant who has yet to start on fruit juices and vegetables. Prunes, sweet potatoes, and apple juice often help the infant who has already started on these foods. If no relief is obtained with these measures or if the constipation is long-lasting, consult your doctor.

Diarrhea refers to stools that are very watery in comparison to normal. A bottle-fed baby's stools will start out as dark and sticky during the first few days of life and proceed to green, yellow, and finally to soft and brown. A baby can have several stools a day or only one every two-three days and still be normal. The consistency and an increase in the number of diarrheal stools over the average, is what is important. An occasional episode is not as serious as continuous, frequent diarrhea, which can cause severe, quick dehydration. A change in the family atmosphere, method of feeding preparation, or formula can lead to diarrhea, as can illness. If your infant is having diarrheal stools, consult your doctor or nurse practitioner immediately so that she can recommend or provide proper rehydration procedures.

Allergies to milk formula are not as common as many parents believe. Often parents attribute spitting-up, vomiting, gas, constipation or diarrhea, and skin rashes to an allergy, without confirmation by a medical person and thereby add more problems to the feeding regimen by changing formulas unnecessarily. If there is a history of asthma, eczema, or any other allergies in the family, infant allergies are more likely.

Infant feeding is an integral part and responsibility of parenthood. It is important not only because it provides nutrition, but also because it is a way in which parents and baby can get to know each other. Despite the advantages of breast-feeding, bottle-feeding can be a nutritious, satisfying experience too.

A Practical Guide To Breast-Feeding Your Baby

by Mary Lu Rang, R.N.

A nurse answers some of the most frequently asked questions about breast-feeding.

What should I do if my baby does not nurse well?

Very few babies nurse well the first few days of life, but try not to become frustrated if your baby is not nursing as eagerly as you would like. It may take at least a month to establish a successful breast-feeding pattern.

You may find it helpful to try different positions when nursing. Whether you lie down or sit, be certain you are comfortable and have the baby positioned safely and securely. His head should be a little higher than his stomach.

Baby's sucking reflex is strongest at the beginning of each feeding, so alternate the breast your baby nurses from first at each feeding. A safety pin attached to your bra strap will help you remember. Gently stroke the corner of the baby's mouth closest to you. He will turn toward you and open his mouth. This is called the "rooting reflex." Then release your fingers and engage the nipple and as much of the areola as possible in the baby's mouth. If your nipples are large and rather flat, it may help to form your nipple between your thumb and index finger or index and middle finger. This will prevent nipple soreness and encourage milk production.

Expressing a few drops of milk onto the baby's mouth and using the rooting reflex will often help a frantically nuzzling baby begin to nurse. Try touching the roof of your baby's mouth with your nipple to stimulate him to suck if he is hesitant to begin nursing. Since babies do not know how to breathe through their mouths, it may be necessary to press down the breast area by his nose so he can breathe easily.

How do I know if I have enough breast milk?

Many nursing mothers are concerned that their babies are not getting an adequate amount of milk. The following are some criteria you may use to judge if your baby's fluid and nutritional needs are being met:

1) Your baby's urine should not be very dark or concentrated. Five or six diaper

changes a day is within normal limits. A breast-fed baby's stool will be loose and gold in color.

2) The anterior fontanel or "soft spot" should be level. If it is depressed, the baby may need more fluid.

3) If your baby has nursed about 15 minutes on each breast and still seems fussy, you can offer a pacifier to satisfy his sucking needs.

4) Your baby's skin should be soft and spring back into place when gently pinched.

5) You can nurse your baby every three or four hours on demand. During growth spurts, you will have to nurse longer or more frequently to satisfy your infant.

6) Ask your doctor if he wants your baby to have water, juice, formula, or some other supplement in addition to breast milk. Most infants thrive on breast-feeding alone. Breast milk is the perfect food for your baby.

7) Many babies have a growth spurt at three weeks, six weeks, and three months of age. These are often the times that mothers stop breast-feeding because the baby will want to nurse very often, and the mother may feel she does not have enough milk. If you allow your baby to nurse on demand, your milk supply will increase in a day or two to satisfy his needs.

Do my breasts and nipples require special care while I am nursing?

Gradually increase the amount of time you nurse over a period of several days. Let your baby's appetite, your milk production, and the condition of your nipples guide you. Many doctors feel that a well-fitting nursing bra will support your breasts and prevent the ligaments from stretching. After nursing, leave the flaps of your nursing bra open about ten minutes to allow your nipples to dry. Your physician may also recommend a lanolin breast cream to lubricate your nipples and help prevent irritation.

Breast pads should be clean and dry. Some mothers use clean, folded, cotton handkerchiefs. Do not use plastic pads or liners because they will keep your nipples wet and promote the growth of bacteria. Wash your hands with soap and water before nursing or expressing milk by hand or with a breast pump. Use only warm water on your nipples. Soap or alcohol products will destroy the anti-infective lubricant produced by the sebaceous glands of the areola (nipple area).

Do not go more than three or four hours without nursing. If you miss a feeding, hand express milk or use a breast pump so the milk ducts do not become blocked. This also helps to maintain your milk supply. Leakage of milk is often preceded by a tingling sensation. To stop leaking milk, press the palm or heel of your hand against your nipple.

When is hand expression useful?

You may want to hand express your milk if:
- Your baby is not latching on to your nipples because of engorgement;
- Your infant did not nurse well, and your breasts are full and uncomfortable;
- You will not be home for a feeding and you want to hand express breast milk into a bottle for your baby;
- Your baby cannot nurse due to prematurity, cracked nipples, or an illness.

How can I hand express my breast milk?

First, wash your hands with soap and water, and cleanse your nipples with warm water. A warm shower or warm cloths placed on your breasts for about ten minutes before expressing your milk will make it easier.

Place one hand under your breast to support it. Next, place your other hand, palm down, on top of your breast. Gently, but firmly, slide your hand down *toward* your nipple. It may help to picture the face of a clock superimposed on your breast as you express your milk. Begin at the 12 o'clock position and repeat these two steps at "every hour" as you move your hands clockwise around the breast.

Place your thumbs above your nipple and your fingers below. Very gently squeeze your fingers and thumb together. Continue to rotate so that you have removed milk from all around the nipple.

Milk production is based on supply and demand. If you are expressing milk because you are engorged, do not remove too much. Your breasts will adjust to your baby's appetite, but it may take a few feedings to do so. If you remove too much milk, your breasts will continue to overproduce.

You can also hand express or pump milk for future use from one breast while your baby nurses from the other. It is much easier since the "letdown" reflex has brought the milk to the nipple area and you just have to pump or express it out.

Do I have to eat anything special or avoid any foods while I am nursing?

Perhaps your physician discussed nutrition with you during your pregnancy. If you feel you should make alterations in your dietary habits, check with your doctor.

If your diet is poor, the quantity of milk your breasts produce is decreased. Breast-feeding increases your needs for almost all the nutrients. As your baby grows, his dietary habits will be modeled on yours.

Eight glasses of water or fluids a day are recommended. Natural juices and water are the best. Carbonated drinks and coffee usually contain caffeine, a drug that may affect your baby through your breast milk.

Never take any medications, even over-the-counter preparations, while nursing, before consulting your doctor. Many drugs are passed into the breast milk and can harm the baby.

When should I wean my baby?

The amount of time it takes to wean your baby depends on your baby's response and your milk supply. Many babies will voluntarily reduce the number of times they breast-feed each day as they get older and mature. Your doctor may suggest that you start introducing solid foods into your baby's diet between six and nine months of age. This may make weaning easier.

Pinpoint the feeding during which your baby is most disinterested. Substitute a bottle or cup at this feeding, and in a week or two, substitute a bottle or cup at another feeding where your baby does not nurse as vigorously. Continue substituting until your baby nurses once a day. By this time you will probably not have much breast milk, and your infant will probably give up this nursing most easily.

What Parents Should Know About Caffeine
by M. Kathleen Doyle Allen, R.D., MEd.

Have you ever noticed that after you've given your child cola for a bedtime snack, your sleepyhead suddenly becomes bright-eyed and alert? There is a good reason for this transformation: your child received a drug that is a strong central nervous system stimulant. The drug is caffeine. When a child drinks a can of cola, the effect of the caffeine is comparable to that of an adult who drinks four cups of coffee—hardly conducive to sleep.

Caffeine As A Drug

Caffeine is a strong central nervous system stimulant. A recent study has shown caffeine to be effective in preventing attention lapses one hour after ingestion of one to two cups of coffee, with the effect lasting three hours. Motor activity is also increased. For example, typists have been found to work faster and with fewer errors after consuming the amount of caffeine in a cup of brewed coffee.

Caffeine, as most of us have noticed after a cup of coffee or tea, is a diuretic, which means that it causes an increased secretion of urine. It also causes an increase in secretion of gastric juices.

Since caffeine is a drug, it can be consumed in toxic doses, causing insomnia, headache, nausea, vomiting, rapid heartbeat, and high blood pressure. Prolonged overindulgence in caffeine beverages results in "caffeinism," with symptoms of restlessness, irritability, and stomach irritation.

How much caffeine is too much? Responses to caffeine are highly individual. One psychiatrist has found symptoms of caffeinism in some persons after ingestion of 250 mg of caffeine, or the amount in approximately two cups of brewed coffee.

Consistent with its properties as a drug, the effects of caffeine are related to body weight. We administer reduced dosages of aspirin or antibiotics to children to achieve the same result as a larger dose for an adult. Yet because of caffeine's presence in our food and drinks, it is easy to overlook the fact that the amount taken by children should be watched carefully. Some pediatricians have expressed concern over caffeinism in children consuming large amounts of cola and chocolate.

Caffeine In Our Food And Drinks

Dietary caffeine is consumed primarily in beverages: coffee, tea, soft drinks, and cocoa. Chocolate candy and chocolate syrup contain caffeine too. Soft drinks contain up to 65 mg per 12 ounce serving; a cup of cocoa contains 10 to 20 mg; and a small chocolate bar may have up to 25 mg of caffeine. The stimulants in tea, cocoa, and chocolate are slightly different chemically from caffeine, but they have the same effects and are referred to as caffeine.

Caffeine content in coffee and tea is a function of the amount of coffee or tea, method of preparation, and length of brewing time. Brewed coffee made by the drip method, including automatic drip coffee makers, contains more caffeine than coffee made in a percolator.

Very strong coffee may contain as much as 330 mg of caffeine per cup. A cup of tea contains 39 to 50 mg; instant ice tea has 20 to 58 mg per 12 ounces.

Caffeine And Pregnancy

Many pregnant women, including formerly avid coffee drinkers, report that they cannot tolerate coffee when experiencing morning sickness and nausea. Some find that coffee no longer appeals to them for the duration of the pregnancy. This is probably because constituents of coffee stimulate the secretion of stomach acids. Even decaffeinated coffee stimulates the stomach secretions to some extent because of the other constituents of the coffee bean.

Caffeine is known to cross the placenta and enter the fetal circulation. The danger of excessive caffeine to the developing fetus is currently the subject of some controversy. Massive doses appear to cause birth defects in animal studies, but effects of smaller quantities have not been satisfactorily examined. Since caffeine is a drug that does reach the fetus, moderate caffeine intake during pregnancy is a wise course of action. A pregnant woman should avoid over-the-counter headache and stay-awake preparations containing caffeine, along with all drugs not prescribed by her doctor.

Lactation And Caffeine

Caffeine taken by a nursing mother reaches the infant through her milk. A moderate intake of caffeine by the breast-feeding mother (for example, one to two cups of coffee) does not appear to have adverse effects on the baby. There have been reports, however, of restless, wakeful babies after the ingestion of large amounts of caffeine by breast-feeding mothers. One mother found that her two-month-old twins started sleeping through the night immediately after she stopped drinking eight glasses of ice tea each day. Although she loved ice tea, she gladly gave it up in exchange for restful nights. It is difficult to say exactly what amount of caffeine intake by the breast-feeding mother might affect her infant, and since the reaction to caffeine is individual, each mother should assess what restriction, if any, should be placed on her ingestion of caffeine beverages.

Nursing mothers who drink coffee, tea, or colas may need to increase their intake of other liquids to compensate for liquid lost because of the diuretic effect of caffeine, which stimulates urination.

Caffeine And Small Children

The same amount of caffeine has a much stronger stimulation effect on a child than on an adult. As most parents would readily testify, small children do not need to be stimulated, so restriction of caffeine beverages, chocolate candy, or colas three hours before naptime and bedtime may contribute to a more peaceful bedtime for children and parents.

A survey showed that about 18 percent of infants under two years consumed some caffeine in a two-week period. In the six- to eleven-month-old group, infants who consumed caffeine received 77 mg per day. This is equivalent to about 19 ounces of cola. This high intake can be accounted for by mothers who give colas to colicky infants. It is ironic that, in an attempt to soothe their infants, these mothers actually produced the opposite effect. The caffeine stimulated the colicky infants, making them wakeful, restless, and perhaps more irritable. Generally, soft drinks should not be given to an infant, especially soft drinks containing caffeine.

The only time a nutritionist might recommend carbonated beverages for a small child is when a clear, liquid diet is necessary during vomiting or diarrhea. At these times soft drinks provide much-needed calories and liquid when other food or drinks might not stay down or could aggravate the illness. If parents prefer to avoid caffeine, they can use carbonated beverages without caffeine: Teem, Seven-up, Sprite, root beer, or ginger ale. They can also check soft drink labels. Since most soft drinks containing caffeine have a caffeine added to that occurring naturally in the kola nut, caffeine will be listed as an ingredient. If caffeine-containing soft drinks are used, they should be served in small amounts several hours before bedtime.

The Slow Spoiler
by William S. Deeley, D.D.S.

The dangers of Nursing Bottle Mouth Syndrome.

Every minute of every hour of every day, some mother is unwittingly contributing to the ruination of her baby's teeth. The weapon is the baby bottle. The ammunition is a high-carbohydrate liquid. The battleground is the crib. Even though the dental profession has repeatedly tried to warn parents of the problem, the incidence of Nursing Bottle Mouth Syndrome (NBMS) remains at the same level year after year.

Nursing Bottle Mouth Syndrome is a condition of rampant decay in a young child's mouth, caused by repeated and prolonged exposure to liquids containing fermentable carbohydrates. This syndrome is the *leading source* of dental problems for children under the age of three years.

How does this problem come about? First of all, from birth to twelve months, the sole source of a child's nourishment is his bottle. After the age of twelve months, the bottle is sometimes used for nighttime or naptime feeding. In order to make the bottle palatable, many parents (and grandparents) use a tasty liquid with a high-carbohydrate concentration. Apple juice, orange juice, grape juice, carbonated beverages, and even milk will break down into decay-causing by-products when in prolonged contact with the oral bacteria.

While NBMS is the scourge of bottle-fed babies, it also occurs in breast-fed infants. Though rare, the documented cases show that the child has slept with the mother and has been breast-fed for long periods of time.

When a naptime or nighttime bottle is used, a definite decay pattern develops. Let's watch David, a hypothetical child (age eighteen months), go to sleep with a bottle of milk and see what happens during the night.

At first wide awake, David sucks eagerly on the bottle. A little while later, when his stomach is nearly full, he becomes drowsy. Shortly thereafter he is asleep with the nipple of the bottle still between his teeth. In sleep the swallowing reflex is diminished and salivary flow decreases. The milk is no longer ingested.

It begins to pool in David's mouth. The milk, containing lactose and rich in carbohydrates, makes a fine feast for the oral bacteria. These bacteria ingest the carbohydrates and lactose and produce acid. This acid is in close contact with the primary (baby) teeth for eight to ten *undisturbed* hours. Repeat this pattern for several weeks, and the acid will begin to erode the enamel of David's teeth, exposing the softer dentin underneath. The process of decay has begun.

This is why, when the condition is first noticed by the parents, the teeth appear to almost "melt away." Decay that rings the back teeth at the gum line is characteristic of this condition. But the lower front teeth may be entirely free of decay. This is probably due to the natural pooling of saliva in this region during sleep. This saliva dilutes the decay-producing liquid and offers some protection. The tongue also covers the lower front teeth during sleep and may also shield these teeth from decay.

Badly decayed upper front teeth are characteristic of NBMS. These teeth, with the nipple of the bottle positioned directly behind them, are the most susceptible to the acid attack. Often these teeth become so decayed that the slightest bump will break them off. It is at this stage that most parents become alarmed because NBMS must now be treated professionally.

Now let's stop for a moment and outline the causes of the problem. First, the type of liquid put into the bottle is important. High-carbohydrate or sugar-containing liquids are the worst offenders. Read the labels on the liquids you feed your baby. Sucrose, dextrose, and corn syrup are all sugars. Apple juice is considered to be the most destructive, although all juices, carbonated beverages, and even milk can contribute to NBMS.

Secondly, the frequency of application is important. All too often, we, as parents, give a child a bottle and a cookie to keep him quiet during a busy day or when company arrives. This unsupervised snacking, with or without a nighttime bottle, can produce the same syndrome.

Now let's consider the child who is already on this nighttime and naptime bottle merry-go-round. How do you, the horrified parent, get him off it? Fear not, there are solutions to the dilemma.

You should ideally feed your child *before* putting him to bed instead of leaving the bottle in the bed. However, if your child is already accustomed to sleeping with the bottle, another approach is necessary.

First of all, don't deprive your child of the bottle altogether. Making him go "cold turkey" will fray his (and your) nerves unnecessarily. Gradually reduce the concentration of the sugary liquid over a period of days by diluting it with water. Continue this treatment until the bottle contains just water. Then the night bottle of water (especially good if the water is fluoridated) can be given until you decide he no longer needs it to sleep.

A third method is to make a substitution. Offer your child a new cuddly toy in exchange for his night bottle. But remember that honesty is the best policy in dealing with children. The "I lost your bottle" approach is definitely not recommended.

The best approach is *prevention*. This means adequate oral hygiene for your baby from the minute you bring him home from the hospital. I am amazed by the number of parents who fail to realize that they can and *should* clean their baby's teeth.

Good oral hygiene can start in the cradle. Even before your newborn has his first tooth, you can clean out his mouth with a moist piece of cotton gauze or a wet washcloth. This should be done after every feeding. Start early, and soon your child will accept and expect this treatment.

This stage of oral hygiene can be continued until the toddler age (eighteen months and up), when parents can introduce the toothbrush in the baby's regimen. Pick a child-size toothbrush with soft bristles. Use it without toothpaste at first.

Soon your child will want to begin brushing his own teeth and should be permitted to try. Most children do not possess the physical coordination to effectively brush their teeth until they are about seven or eight years old. This means that parents should check and *re-brush* a child's teeth until that age.

Professional care of a baby with NBMS is usually extensive and expensive. This care often has to be rendered by a dentist who specializes in the treatment of children, a pedodontist. Slight cases can be treated by remineralization, hardening the softer, decayed parts of the baby teeth with topical treatments of fluorides, in conjunction with routine dental care.

Severe cases may require a wide range of dental services. The individual patient may require fillings, extractions, root canal treatments, interceptive orthodontics, chrome steel crowns for molars, and plastic crowns for incisors. In short, the entire primary dentition (all of the baby teeth) must be restored to ensure that the health of the child and the development of the adult dentition is unaffected.

But the saddest fact of all is that Nursing Bottle Mouth Syndrome is entirely *preventable*. A little knowledge can make a world of difference.

Primer For Fathers

Some fathers face the prospect of bathing and diapering their babies with genuine alarm. But all it takes is a little practice, and in no time you'll be an old hand at all the basics of baby care. Here, one new father shows you how.

How To Pick Up And Put Down A Baby

An important point to remember is never to pick up your baby without first alerting her to your presence by either talking to her or touching her. Particularly if your baby is sleeping on her stomach, she needs to know you're there before you suddenly swoop her up in the air.

If she is sleeping on her stomach, put your left hand under her neck and your right hand under her bottom. Spread your fingers to help support her head and thighs. Lean down so that your left wrist and forearm follow her spine right down to her waist level. If she is sleeping on her back, use one hand to support her head, with your arm across her shoulders. The young baby can't yet hold up her head, so without your support, the head might snap back and this could

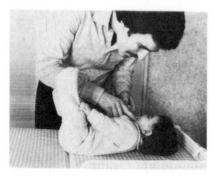

"An important point to remember is never to pick up your baby without first alerting her to your presence by either talking to her or touching her."

cause injury. Swing your other arm around baby and grasp her firmly around the middle. All your movements should be slow and gentle; though a baby is not made of glass, rough handling will, at the very least, probably startle her.

To put her down, slowly lower her until her head and back are on your left hand and arm resting on the mattress. Lower her bottom. When it, too, is supported, gently slide your hands out from under her.

How To Diaper Baby

First make sure that the baby is on a firm surface—a changing table or on a towel on a firm bed. Unfasten the soiled diaper. For easy maneuvering of squirmy babies, hold the baby's legs up by grasping both ankles with one hand. Thoroughly cleanse the bottom, in and around all the creases. (But be careful if your baby decides to "go" just then.) Place the clean diaper under the baby (back of diaper should be at the baby's waist). Pull the front of the diaper up between the baby's legs, smoothing out the bunches. If there is extra fabric or material, tuck it in where the baby needs extra padding—in the front for a boy or a girl who sleeps on her stomach; in the rear if she sleeps on her back. To pin a cloth diaper, slip two fingers between the baby and the diaper to keep from sticking the baby. For disposable diapers, make sure the plastic liner is tucked in. The tape tabs fasten from back to front.

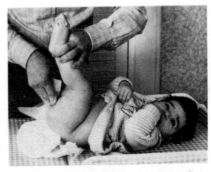
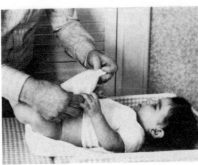
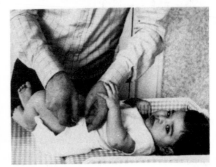

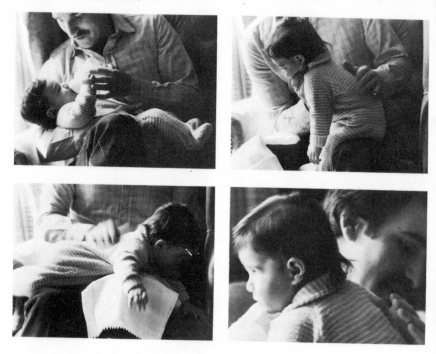

Feeding And Burping Your Baby:

Select a comfortable chair for feeding and sit with your baby cradled in your arms. Test a drop of formula on the inside of your wrist. It should be room temperature or even slightly cold. Keep the bottle tilted up so the nipple is always full, but stop at once if the baby starts gagging.

Some babies swallow a lot of air and may need to be burped several times during the feeding. One method of burping recommended for the newborn is to sit the baby on your knee, face down, and place your hand just under the collarbone. Massage the baby's back gently using a rotating motion until the bubble comes up. Another position is to lay the baby across your legs, on her stomach. A burp in this position, however, will probably bring milk with it as the air cannot rise above the milk level. For an older baby, the best position is to stretch out the baby along the side of your body so that she is straight and upright. Her head will rest right on your shoulder, and to help her get up the bubble, rub, pat or massage her back. Be sure to protect your clothing with a diaper or cloth.

Bathing Your Baby

Your baby can be bathed in a special baby bath or in the kitchen sink. If you use the sink, wrap the faucet with a cloth so that the baby won't be accidentally hit

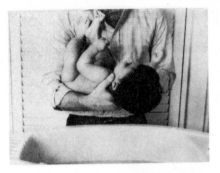

"A good rule of thumb is to wash the baby from the cleanest part of her body to the most soiled: that means face first, genitals last."

by the faucet. Line the sink with a cloth diaper or other cloth so the baby won't slip. The water should be comfortably warm, and you don't need too much of it.

To place baby in the tub, support her head and shoulders and grasp her far arm at the shoulder using a firm grip. Support her buttocks with your other hand, grasping the far leg at the thigh. Slide baby into the water slowly, feet first, to avoid frightening her.

A good rule of thumb is to wash the baby from the cleanest part of her body to the most soiled: that means face first, genitals last. Always use gentle motions. When wiping the eye, wipe from the inner corner outwards. Wipe around ears and neck to get rid of dried sweat that might cause soreness. Clean around her mouth and chin creases to remove dried milk and dribble. Wipe each hand, checking for any sharp fingernails that might need to be trimmed. Then clean all around the buttocks and into the creases.

The football hold is handy for rinsing baby's head: support the head and back with one hand, with baby's body along your arm and her legs in the crease of your arm. This leaves you a free hand to rinse the baby's head while holding it over the tub. Finally, gently remove the baby from the tub and put her on a bath pad or towel. Cover her with the towel while you thoroughly and gently dry all the creases.

Living (And Coping) With Colic
by Jane Hunter Imber

Molly's birth was everything I had hoped it would be, and her father and I marveled at the new life we had created. We were delighted that she was so alert, and even her crying was music to our ears.

The first week of Molly's life, her grandmother was with us to help out. Molly cried much of the time, but we were able to cope quite well. Despite our sleepless nights, during the day we could pass her to another adult and get some much needed rest. But the first week we were on our own, we quickly discovered that it was impossible to sleep—night or day—because our baby was rarely quiet. We learned that we had a colicky baby.

Colic, fretfulness, irritable crying—whatever it's called—sounds the same. In many, but not all, babies it is associated with abdominal pain and intestinal gas. The cause of colic is not known although there are several theories. However, its most striking characteristic is the piercing screams an infant makes for hours at a time.

We had thought we were prepared for a baby. We knew that children cried, that newborns were often awake at night, that the first few weeks would be especially difficult, and so forth. What we did not know was how irritating, anger-provoking, and frustrating a colicky baby could be. Only after we started describing Molly's temperament to other people did we realize how common her condition is.

How did we survive? When Molly has a fussy time now and I feel my anger rising, I wonder how we lived through the period when there seemed to be no break in the screaming. Yet we did manage, and as our pediatrician predicted, the colic subsided when Molly was three months old.

The following are some suggestions that helped us survive. I only wish we had been more knowledgeable about colic before her birth.

Ignore Well-Meaning Remarks

After we had been assured by our pediatrician that Molly was thriving physically, we began to accept her screaming as something that we had to live with temporarily. However, to most outsiders, especially those without children and those who only knew "good" babies, it seemed impossible that an infant would cry as she did unless there was something seriously wrong. We found it very difficult to ignore their well-intended remarks, but we had to. For every bit of advice we received from one person, we heard exactly the opposite from someone else. "Oh, you're breast-feeding? She's obviously not getting enough milk." "You must have too much milk for her." "Your milk is too rich (or too thin)." "You should (should not) be giving her water (or using a pacifier)," and so on. My advice is that if it's at all possible, smile and change the subject. Listen to your pediatrician, but forget the advice of others.

Do Whatever Works

Do the things that seem to comfort your baby. If it means feeding her more frequently than scheduled, do it. (We did try to make Molly go a minimum of two hours between feedings, but there were still times when we cheated.) If it means letting her sleep with you at night, fine. If it means holding her through her naps, that's OK too. If it works, do it. Don't worry that by "giving in" you'll be spoiling her. Right now you need whatever peace and quiet you can get. Besides, most authorities feel it is impossible to spoil very young babies.

Take Frequent Breaks

No matter how good your motives are, it doesn't help to punish yourself because your infant has colic. It's imperative for your mental and physical health to maintain contact with the outside world. Every couple of weeks we asked an understanding friend to sit with Molly while we went out together for an hour or two. Also each day we made it a point for one of us to stay with Molly while the other took a walk. Or one of us would take Molly for a drive while the other enjoyed the luxury of a quiet home.

Recognize And Accept Your Feelings

I really wanted to be the model mother—the one all of us have read about on Mother's Day—patient, understanding, wise. Yet I snapped at my husband, cried with my daughter, and hated myself for the way I felt. There were many days when I was angry and resentful of my child (Why aren't you the way babies are supposed to be?), times when I was frustrated to the point of tears (I've rocked you and listened to you for hours, now shut up!), and times when I feared I might physically hurt her if I didn't put her down and get away from the screams. At these times the best thing for me, and for Molly, was to give her to someone else, or, if no one was home, put her in her crib and escape, even if only to the next room.

It's amazing how reassuring it can be to find someone who really understands what you're going through. Not only does it remind you that you aren't the only person in the world who has a colicky baby, but it helps you realize that eventually an infant outgrows it. And if your friend has survived a colicky baby, of course you can too.

Invest In Special Products

These are the items we found indispensable. Nothing worked all of the time, but these worked often enough to be valuable.

A pacifier: Colicky babies often need something to suck. We purchased several and kept them strategically placed throughout the house, which helped prevent frantic searching when the baby was crying at the top of her lungs.

A soft front-carrying baby carrier. A soft carrier holds the baby in close physical contact with the wearer. This was often the only way Molly would sleep, and it freed my hand for reading and simple household tasks.

A carriage. Although an old-fashioned baby buggy with cushioned springs can be a big investment if you buy it new, it may be possible to borrow one or purchase it secondhand. We found ours an invaluable aid in helping Molly nap and getting us both out of the house and into the fresh air. And when the baby is crying, it never sounds as loud outdoors as it does when it echoes throughout the house.

"Lullaby From The Womb"

Dr. Hajime Murooka has developed and tested this recording of uterine sounds on several crying newborns and has had dramatic results. I found that at times Molly was really comforted by the record, and as she grew older, we both enjoyed the classical lullabies on the other side (available from Capital records—ST-11421).

Finally, and most important, don't give up—babies do outgrow colic. When Molly was two weeks old and our pediatrician told us she would outgrow her irritability by three months, our first thought was, "Ten more weeks of this?" However, we survived, and the time did pass. It would be incorrect to say we enjoyed Molly's first few months, but nonetheless, there were moments we still cherish. And as the colic subsided, we discovered a truly delightful, lovable, and happy child.

Your Newborn's Needs
And How to Meet Them
by Dr. Alvin N. Eden

There is no question that a new baby brings some real changes into your life. You are now in an entirely new "ball game" that should bring much joy and happiness into your home. It must not and need not become a time of undue tension and worry. Unfortunately, many new parents are totally unprepared for what to expect from their newborn. This results in harried, harassed, and tired mothers and fathers who have very little time or energy left over to enjoy their new babies or to enjoy each other.

As a pediatrician, I know full well how important the first few months of a baby's life are in establishing the proper patterns of behavior and personality. Everyone agrees that infants flourish and thrive in relaxed and peaceful households (as do their parents). The purpose of this article is to teach you what the new baby is all about. This knowledge should make your job easier and more pleasant.

Whether we like it or not, a new baby is a lot of work. There are many more new chores to be done. Obviously this leaves less time for the usual pre-infant activities. Nobody can do it all. To be able to properly cope with the job at hand, a new order of priorities must be established. This requires a bit of planning and organization. For example, cuddling and holding your baby should rank ahead of a clean kitchen floor. Let some of the housework go—a happy and contented infant is more important than a freshly vacuumed rug.

How does the new baby generally behave?

Briefly, new babies "startle" frequently and cry a good deal of the time. They grunt and grimace and squirm and kick. They often breathe noisily and irregularly.

Can a newborn hear?

Yes, right from birth.

When can my baby begin to see?

Studies have shown that newborns' eyes react at birth, but they cannot focus at all until about two weeks of age. By four weeks they can focus on large objects and bright lights, and begin to follow up on the midline of the visual field. During the first month the eyes cross frequently, and this is no cause for concern.

The new baby is so small. Is he weak and fragile?

On the contrary, infants are strong and vigorous. They are small all right, but remarkably well-engineered and well-designed. They are meant to be handled, held, fondled, and kissed, not just looked at. The more close contact the better. Just remember that the newborn's head is a bit wobbly for the first couple of months and needs to be supported when he is picked up or held. By one month of age, the infant can raise his head while lying on his stomach.

Can a new baby be taken out of doors?

Certainly, as long as the weather is reasonably good. I would suggest that you avoid crowds when you do take him out. There is no point in increasing his risk of exposure to illness.

How about visitors?

By all means. But they should not be allowed to cough or breathe all over the baby. These are sure ways of spreading colds and other respiratory infections. If your visitors insist on kissing the new addition, make sure it is not on the baby's mouth.

When can I bathe my new baby?

Just as soon as the umbilical cord has fallen off. (Usually, this takes about a week. Until the cord is off, I suggest that you sponge bathe the baby. Daily baths are not absolutely necessary. However, most babies do get to enjoy the bath, so if at all possible, it is a good idea to bathe the baby often.

Is it necessary for a mother to always stay with her baby?

Absolutely not. Take some time out and get away from the infant—for an hour, an afternoon—as long as you make arrangements to have reliable substitute care for the baby. Get out of the house when you can. Not only are these outings good for you, but in the long run they will be good for your baby. Even when you are at home, it is not necessary to constantly hover over the baby, looking for trouble. The infant will let you know soon enough if he has any problems.

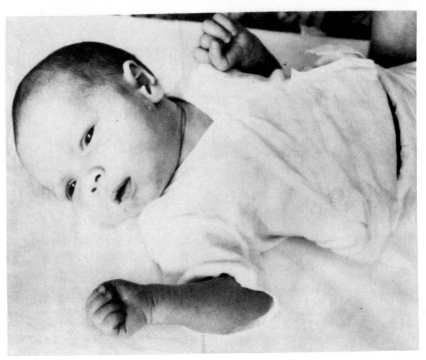

How about weight gain?

Most newborns lose some weight while in the hospital nursery. They come home weighing less than their birthweight, and by ten days of age, they are usually back to their original weight. During the first month, the usual total weight gain is between one and 1-1/2 pounds. I do not recommend that you have an infant scale at home. Weighing your baby can wait until the first checkup at your doctor's office.

How much does a baby grow during the first month?

An average of one inch.

Is the new baby drinking enough milk?

If he is content most of the time and gaining weight satisfactorily, then he is getting enough. The normal baby's desire and capacity take care of his individual needs. The new baby usually takes a feeding every three or four hours. If the baby is fussy or crying less than three hours after the last feeding, give him some water or a pacifier, since it is unlikely that he is hungry.

How about sleep?

This is actually a two-part question—about your sleep and the baby's sleep. With rare exceptions, you, the parent, will now be getting less uninterrupted sleep than before. This will lead, sooner or later, to fatigue and increased irritability. But there is a simple remedy for this. Learn to lie down and rest during the day while the baby is sleeping.

During the first month of his life, the baby sleeps lightly and moves around a good deal while asleep. He is easily awakened, so it is a good idea to keep the noise level down a bit while he sleeps.

Very few infants sleep through the night during the first four weeks. They usually wake up every three or four hours, ready to be changed and fed. There is no way to avoid these feedings. I would suggest to you that there is no law that requires mama to always be the night feeder. Papa can also get into the act. The obvious exception is breast-feeding. But the duties and chores can be shared between mother and father.

What about urine and bowel movements?

If you had a quarter for every time your baby had a wet diaper, you would be wealthy in no time. Infants are almost continuously wet, and this is normal. If your new baby remains dry for the entire day or the entire night, this would be unusual, and your doctor should be notified. As for bowel movements, my best advice is not to count them. Some infants normally have one bowel movement every two or three days, while others have a bowel movement after each feeding. What is important is that the bowel movements be normal in consistency—that is, not too watery—and they do not contain blood or mucus. It is common for infants to strain and grunt with each bowel movement, and you need not worry or do anything about this. Occasionally if the grunting and straining become very severe, flexing the baby's legs will help him pass his stool. What you should remember is that any significant change in the usual pattern of your baby's urine or bowel movements should be reported to your doctor.

How much crying should you expect?

This, of course, varies from baby to baby. Some hardly cry at all, and others are more irritable and cry a great deal of the time. But it's safe to say that all new babies do some crying, and this is considered perfectly normal. I should like to emphasize that babies cry for reasons other than being hungry. Sometimes they are simply thirsty for water, are wet, or gassy, or just plain cranky without explanation. It takes some experience, but many parents learn to differentiate the various types of crying after a few weeks.

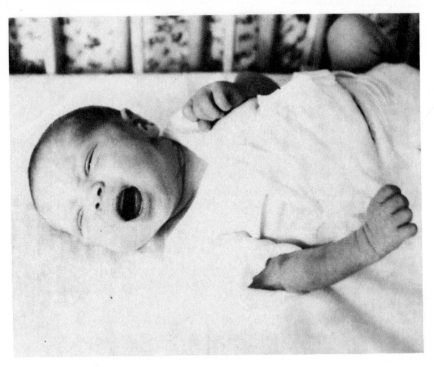

What are some common "problems" that are not "problems"?

1. Sneezing and hiccuping: These occur frequently, are considered normal, and require no treatment.

2. Mottling (marbleized spots) of the skin when the baby's clothes are removed: absolutely normal.

3. Diaper rashes and heat rashes: Very few babies get through the first month without one kind of rash or another. There is no reason for you to feel guilty if your baby develops a diaper rash. To help prevent rashes, I advise that you keep the baby cool and comfortable and that you change his wet and dirty diapers as promptly as possible.

4. Mucus in the corners of the eyes and in the nose and wax in the ears: All this should be expected. I suggest that you clean these areas carefully and not too vigorously.

5. Cradle cap in the scalp: This is a yellowish crusting commonly seen during the first month and is no cause for alarm. Oil and a fine-tooth comb work well in getting rid of cradle cap.

When should your doctor be called?

1. Forceful or projectile vomiting: If, instead of the usual spitting-up or cheesing, the baby vomits large amounts of his feedings.

2. Diarrhea: If the bowel movements become more watery and more frequent than usual.

3. Poor feeding: If your baby stops his usual vigorous sucking during his feedings.

4. Different type of crying: If your baby suddenly starts and continues to cry, and the cry is not his usual kind.

5. Any significant change in your baby's usual color, breathing, behavior, or activity.

My husband thinks that it is unmanly to change our baby's diapers. How can I convince him otherwise?

There is no question that many of us have been brainwashed to believe that it is somehow not masculine for a father to change diapers or for that matter to bathe or even feed the baby. This is utter nonsense. I believe that just the opposite is true. It is not manly for a father to abdicate his role and to just stand by and watch. Your husband must be convinced that you need his help and more important, that the baby needs his day-to-day participation as well.

Many mothers automatically take over the entire job of caring for the baby. This results in an overly tired and harried woman who has not time or strength left for her husband, and this can obviously lead to marital stresses. New mothers and fathers must learn to share their new chores and responsibilities.

What are good signs of a healthy baby?

If your baby sucks the bottle (or breast) vigorously, cries lustily, and has a good healthy color, chances are excellent that he is fine.

This completes what I have to say about the new baby. You should now have a pretty good idea about what to expect during the first month. If you are ever in doubt or really worried about your baby's behavior, do not hesitate to call your doctor.

When There's More Than One

by Marilyn McGinnis

A mother of twins shares ten ways to cope with a multiple birth.

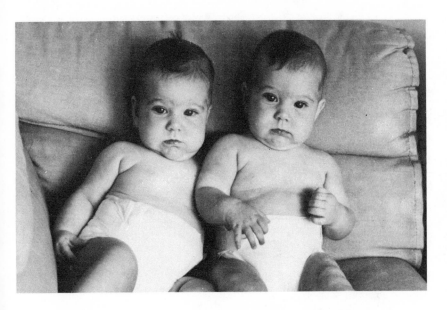

"It's a boy," the doctor said matter-of-factly, pulling tiny Jonathan from the gaping hole in my abdomen.

"That's great!" I beamed happily, straining for the first glimpse of my little son. "My husband will be so happy!"

But the doctor wasn't finished speaking. And his next words were to change the entire course of our lives.

"There's someone else in there," he continued calmly. "It's a boy too."

A week after the boys were born, as my husband and I began slowly emerging from a state of shock, the realities of life with twins and a two-year-old daughter began to hit us. "All you'll do is babies for a year," people told us, and they were right. Before that year was over, we were changing just under 300 diapers a week, and feeding time seemed like a 24-hour marathon. Having now survived that year, perhaps these pointers will help you or someone you know through the first few months with twins.

Don't be afraid to ask for help. The work load for twins is three or four times greater than for one baby. Unless you have a relative nearby to help you regularly, you probably should hire at least part-time help.

A whole host of people paraded through our home the first year, bringing us home-cooked meals, watching the children while I ran errands or slept, and doing our grocery shopping. Until the boys were sleeping through the night, we hired a neighbor to spend two nights a week at our house so I could get a full night of sleep. When the boys were eight months old—and I had reached the point of exhaustion—we hired a high-school girl to help after school. (I should have done it much sooner.) A wonderful grandmother from our church comes one day a week now so I can get out of the house.

If she had it to do over again, reflects one mother of three-year-old twin boys, "I'd take out a loan if necessary to get more help during the first year."

Put the babies on the same schedule. Babies generally set their own schedules for eating and sleeping, but two babies may set two different schedules. I soon learned the value of feeding, changing, and bathing both babies at the same time. Otherwise, you will be feeding babies constantly right around the clock.

One of the joys of feeding time is being able to hold your baby close as you nurse or give him a bottle. This becomes more difficult when there are two. I've met a number of mothers who successfully nursed their twins, sometimes even both at the same time. Since ours were bottle-fed, my husband and I tried to keep up the body contact by sitting on the couch with one baby lying on each side of us up against our legs while we held their bottles. You can also feed them in their infant seats, especially when it's time to start solids. Keep paper and pencil handy to record feeding time and the amount of food and formula each baby takes so there is no doubt in your mind who has eaten what. When you start solids, using one spoon and one dish (unless they are sick) is much easier than trying to juggle two.

A few special pieces of equipment are well worth the investment. A *double stroller* is an expensive item, but without it you're really housebound. The new face-to-face models are the width of a normal stroller, making it relatively easy to get them through doorways and down the aisles of stores. They can also double as a highchair when you go visiting. *Car seats,* too, are a must for safety when you travel.

When your twins reach the into-everything-crawler/toddler age, the portable expanding *Kiddie Corral* will be of help. I have one that expands from an easy-to-carry 12″ diameter cylinder to 12-1/2′. (It's also available in 8′ and 15′ diameter.) With the Corral you can take your toddlers out in the yard—or into people's homes—without fear that they will pull up flowers or knock over vases.

Don't neglect other brothers and sisters. Our daughter had been the star attraction for 22 months when the boys were born. But suddenly her world changed as drastically as ours. Her demands for attention, once met fairly quickly, were now met regularly with, "Just a minute, honey. I'm changing (or feeding) the babies."

I tried to allow some time during the day (often only a few minutes) for the two of us to be alone, and gradually she began to catch on. One day as I was sitting on the couch feeding the boys, she was particularly persistent.

"Mommy, help me with this puzzle," she repeated over and over. Since I was holding two bottles at the time, all I could do was tell her that I could watch her put the puzzle together, but I couldn't help. Still she kept demanding my help until in utter exhaustion, I set down the bottles and leaned back on the couch thinking, "This is all a mistake. I'm just not cut out for motherhood."

To my surprise and delight, Shana threw herself across me and exclaimed, "Oh, now it's Shana's turn. I love you!"

Another problem for the sibling of twins is the amount of attention that the twins get from others. People often stop to admire a new baby, but twice as many people (it seems) stop to admire twins. And they often thoughtlessly ignore the other children in the family. Alert friends and relatives ahead of time to greet your other children first and then the new little ones.

Take time for yourself. If it's a choice between sitting down to read a magazine or doing a load of diapers because there will be no clean ones in the morning if you don't, what should you do? The diapers, of course. Yet continually short-changing yourself on time alone will take its toll.

Unless you have regular help, at best you will only have *moments* of solitude. Make the most of those moments. During her first year with boy/girl twins, Linda's husband left for work a half-hour before her children woke up. She used that 30 minutes to shower, dress, and quietly prepare herself for the day.

Take time for your husband and your marriage. A small baby puts a strain on any marriage. Two babies put a double strain. It's important to remember that you and your husband came first.

Early in the game we saved Friday nights out for ourselves. When your anniversary rolls around, suggest to the grandparents that the best possible present would be free baby-sitting for a weekend so you and your husband can get away.

Simplify housework and shopping. Most people do not expect you to keep a perfect house when you have small children. If you cannot afford a housekeeper, simplify housework as much as possible. Use paper plates to cut down on dirty dishes. Save major housecleaning chores for next year. By the time your babies reach the one-year mark, you'll find yourself with much more time for housework. It's unlikely your house will have collapsed into rubble in the meantime.

Locate the drive-ins near you: banks, cleaners, dairies, restaurants. It will give you a feeling of freedom (and save time) if you can handle chores from your car without loading and unloading the babies.

Find another mother of twins with whom you can share problems and solutions. When you're having a particularly difficult day, it's a great help to be able to call another mother of twins and unload a little. Recognizing the unique needs of mothers of twins, the National Organization of Mothers of Twins Clubs, Inc., was formed a number of years ago. Local chapters meet monthly in numerous areas all across the country. Some of the meetings feature special speakers such as pediatricians, psychologists, and nutritionists discussing the nature and needs of twins. There is also a clothing and equipment exchange and time to share problems and solutions with the other mothers. For the location of the club nearest you, ask your pediatrician or write to the MOTC headquarters at 5402 Amberwood Lane, Rockville, Maryland 20853.

Record each "first" in their baby books as diligently as you did for your other children. Write things down on a slip of paper as soon as they happen or you may frequently find yourself saying, "One of the twins did such and such—forget which." Put the papers in a safe place, and record them in the baby books when you have more time.

Take time to appreciate your wonderful double blessing. Watching two babies of exactly the same age grow and develop is a unique experience. Enjoy their similarities. Appreciate their differences. Know that you are not a mother of twins by chance. The theme of the Mothers of Twins Clubs is "Where God Chooses the Members."

Before I left the hospital with our two tiny bundles, a kind doctor gave me some mimeographed sheets of suggestions for mothers of twins. The last statement on the last page sums up life for a mother of twins:

"You will often wish there were two of you, but you will never wish there were only one of them."

Chapter 3
Growth and Development

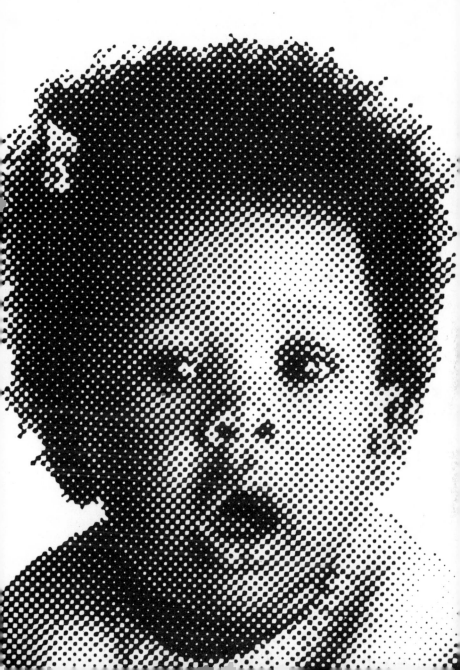

How Babies Learn To Talk

by Dr. Harris D. Riley, Jr., and Joan M. Berney, R.N.

From babbling syllables to words, your child finally becomes skilled at language. Here is how his speech develops and how you can aid the process.

We humans are a talkative lot. We talk to each other and about each other. We talk about our experiences and our dreams. Most of us talk, whether we have anything to say or not.

Tom and Cindy Gallagher were no exception. When their son, Jason, was born, they expressed their joy with words. Jason himself had only one immediate comment on the matter. He opened his mouth and gave a loud, lusty howl. Perhaps he was saying, "Here I am world!"

Maturation of a child's speech and language normally keeps pace with his total maturation and follows a fairly predictable pattern up to the age of about six years. The early stages of speech and language development reflect the child's reception of speech sounds and are revealed by his response to them. Comprehension of language develops more rapidly than the ability to verbalize. Almost from the beginning a child is able to understand many more words and more complicated combinations than he can use. This remains true until his adult speech pattern is established.

Birth To Two Months

Actually, a healthy baby's first cry does more to aerate his lungs than to communicate his thoughts. He soon begins, however, to use crying as a means of getting what he needs. He wakes up wet and hungry; he screams. In no time at all, his mother appears with food, dry diapers, and tender cuddling. It is a noisy but effective means of communication.

As you might expect from one with so little practice, baby's early crying is pretty monotonous. Sometimes loud, sometimes very loud, he always uses the same note. At this point, he's able to communicate only one idea—discomfort. Gradually his cry becomes more versatile. Angry yelling and sucking noises mean it's time to eat. A high-pitched scream is his distress call; perhaps he's having gas pains. Low-pitched crying with sighs and yawns means he's sleepy. A baby quickly learns to use his vocal apparatus for more than mere crying. Jason was less than a month old when he began to gurgle, sigh, and coo. It didn't sound like much, but he was making many of the vowel and consonant sounds that would later be put together into words.

Two To Five Months

At about two or three months, a baby begins to experiment with all sorts of noises. Speech experts call it babbling. The babbling infant uses some recognizable English vowels and consonants, of course. But he also throws in a good dollop of French and Swahili. Human beings can produce an unlimited number of sounds, and a baby sees no reason to restrict himself to one language at this point.

Babbling often occurs when the baby is alone. Then, when he sees or hears his mother, he may revert to his crying language to get her to pick him up. One way to encourage speech growth at this stage is to delay going to the baby when he's alone, contented, and amusing himself with babbling. It's also good to spend time talking with him when he's fed and relaxed. But don't monopolize the conversation. Give him a few gentle words, smile, and wait for his "reply."

Five To Seven Months

At five months a baby is a bundle of constant motion. The continual kicking and flailing help him learn to use his body. By now he's practicing almost as ceaselessly with his voice. He's learning to manipulate his lips, tongue, and breathing in order to produce sound.

A six-month-old baby is a very social creature. He's fascinated with the art of conversation. When adults are talking with each other, he often stops his own perpetual motion to watch the speaker intently.

His speech still consists of babbling, but now he prefers to babble socially rather than alone. When someone talks to him, he smiles and makes an answering noise. He may try to initiate some of the sounds he hears, but he isn't able to say actual words yet.

This is when babies begin using double syllables or combinations. *Ma-ma* or *da-da* are favorites, much to the delight of his parents. Frequently, a baby will choose one such double syllable, perhaps *ma-ma*, and practice it to the exclusion of all others for days or weeks at a time. Speech experts maintain that a six-month-old baby's *ma-ma* is not a true word. The mama in question would probably argue with them.

Eight Months To One Year

Before a baby can learn to talk, he must understand what it is he wants to say. An eight- or nine-month-old child is beginning to comprehend a lot of what is going on around him. Jason is a good example. When he was eight months old, he still screamed loud and long when he felt he was on the verge of starvation. But when he saw his mother approaching with a bottle, he knew that help was on the way. He would instantly stop crying and reach out his arms in anticipation.

By nine months or so, a baby's babbling begins to take on the rhythm and inflection of his native tongue. It's all gibberish, of course, but now it sounds as if he's asking a question or making a profound statement.

His imitation becomes more purposeful too. Baby says *"ma-ma,"* and his mother answers, *"ma-ma."* He's likely to repeat the syllables back to her. His mother loves it. She laughs and says, *"ma-ma"* once more. Baby replies, *"ma-ma."* What fun! He and the most important person in his life are making the same pleasant sound! At the same time he also begins to attempt to imitate facial expressions and formation of sounds on the lips of people who talk to him.

This kind of play is very good speech practice. Listen to the baby's sounds and inflections, and try to mimic him. Hearing an adult mimic him shows the baby that he's on the right track.

The entire first year is ideally a "vocal play" period in which the child learns to enjoy making vocal noises, has them pleasantly reinforced, and becomes able to discriminate among and make use of particular combinations for his own benefit. From these early few meaningful combinations, vocabulary develops by extension of the process, and new meanings become associated with the repetition of other combinations, which lead to fulfillment of other needs.

At ten to twelve months, through these processes of a discriminative babbling, changes of pitch, and imitation of visual and hearing combinations, the child begins to discover that particular combinations repeated often enough will bring about certain desirable ends. Usually among the earliest discoveries is that the combination *ma-ma* will bring his mother to pay some attention to him. By twelve months most infants are using at least one to three such combinations in a meaningful way.

Somewhere between ten and eighteen months, the average child will utter his first true word. That word usually crystallizes from the back-and-forth imitation between mother and baby that he began to enjoy at about eight months. Now, however, he uses the word or combination in a meaningful way. When he wants his mother, he calls out his magic word, *mama.* Real speech has begun.

Although the vocabulary of the one-year-old usually consists of no more than three words, he is able to communicate a variety of wants and emotions. He relies heavily on gestures. He points to the toy he wants. He asks to be picked up by raising his arms when mom or dad comes into the room. He pushes the spoon away when it contains pureed beets.

At eighteen months, a child has a limited, rudimentary command of English. His pronunciation and connotation leave a little to be desired, but he's able to speak his mind to family members who understand his lingo. He has names for people, objects, and activities. He uses one-word sentences. *Dink* may mean, "I'm thirsty, I need a glass of something wet." His sister Janet is *Anneh. Ait* means, "Turn on the light."

Babbling becomes jargon. He converses endlessly in this strange Martian language with the inflection and punctuation of fluent English. He'll talk to anyone who'll listen: mom, dad, or his teddy bear. He is actually rehearsing the art of conversation.

The best way to help your child's speech growth at this time is to talk to him. Talk about what you are doing: "Now it's time for lunch. First, I'll pour the milk into Lisa's glass. Now I'll pour a glass for me. Next, we'll serve the soup."

Talking in this way about the events and surroundings of daily life creates companionship between a mother and her child. It also helps the child learn words, phrases, and sentence construction. Between eighteen months and two years of age, a child's vocabulary grows with incredible speed. He may learn as many as 250 words in this short time.

By the time he's two, the average child can get his point across without much trouble. Gradually he abandons his jargon in favor of simple sentences. "Milk aw gone." "Dad go work." "Baby cry."

At the age of three, about 90 percent of a child's speech is at least understandable. He makes mistakes, mispronounces words, and substitutes easier consonants for the more difficult ones. *L, s, z, r, gr, st,* and *ch* are some of the sounds he might have trouble with.

Correcting is best done obliquely. When he mispronounces a word, use the word yourself in normal conversation. Say it slowly and distinctly. Never correct mistakes in anger.

There are literally hundreds of languages in this world. No matter which one they are learning, all normal babies master the art of talking at about the same rate. And they do it by following the same basic steps. So enjoy each part of your baby's speech learning process. It's all part of the adventure of growing up.

The Astonishing Newborn
by Karen Lohela Woodworth

Anne and Dave gaze lovingly at their newborn. The baby returns their gaze steadily. "Does he really see us?" they wonder, "or are we just a formless blur to him?"

Anne and Dave are not alone in wondering how well their baby can see. Scientists, too, have long been curious about the mysterious world of newborns. How much *can* they see and hear? Are they aware of people and happenings around them, or are they oblivious to their surroundings?

Since babies can't communicate, research on infant perception and mental development has been difficult. But thanks to sophisticated techniques developed recently for studying babies' abilities, we are learning more about newborns. And what we are learning about their capabilities and responsiveness is astonishing.

How do we go about measuring a baby's mental abilities? Most researchers have focused on measuring the infant's *sensory* abilities as an indication of how much information babies can acquire about their world. The results indicate that the perception is keener than we thought.

Sensory Abilities

Newborn babies actually take in, or perceive, a great deal of their world, much more than was previously thought possible. Their brain and all five senses are relatively well developed at birth.

Vision. A newborn baby clearly sees objects 8 to 12 inches from his eyes. When a bright object is moved across his field of vision, he will focus on it and track its movements with his gaze. Estimates of the newborn's visual acuity range from a surprisingly good 20/150 to 20/400, and this improves steadily as he matures. By 14 weeks of age, he can see objects several yards away.

By two months of age, babies develop the eye coordination necessary for depth perception and can tell the difference between certain colors and between different degrees of brightness. A newborn's sight will not fully mature for many months. But what he can already see at birth is amazing when we consider that, in the past, it was thought that newborns couldn't focus their eyes at all and really didn't see anything.

Investigators studying infant vision and attention have found that even one-week-old infants can differentiate between varying shapes and patterns. This involves complex mental processes: first seeing the shapes and then recognizing their differences. How do we know babies can perceive the difference between, for example, a circle and a square? Because they have favorites! Babies prefer to look, for example, at curved rather than linear forms and at horizontal rather than vertical patterns.

One major advance that made such research possible was the development of the visual preference test for infants by Dr. Robert Fantz at Case Western Reserve University in 1958. His test involved showing two pictures to an infant, which are placed inside a darkened box-like apparatus, and then measuring how long the infant looks at each picture. The picture being viewed by the infant is reflected in his eyes, over the center of the cornea. The examiner can see and record this photographically. When a baby prefers to spend more time looking at one picture than the other, he clearly not only sees them but also tells them apart.

Using the visual preference test, Dr. Fantz discovered that babies will look longer at patterns similar to the human face than at other objects. Other studies, too, have suggested that babies pay a lot of attention to faces and that their growing perception of faces is an important part of their social development.

At first, babies don't see a face as an adult does. Though we don't yet know at exactly what age babies can first recognize a face, studies have indicated that initially they are attracted to and look mostly at just the outer contours of a face. By the second month babies begin to look more at the eyes and other internal features of the face. Subseqently they learn to perceive the individual facial features as being related parts of a whole—a face.

Hearing. Babies are able to hear at birth, but their hearing is not yet very sensitive or acute. They can hear sounds of medium intensity, like a voice, and can distinguish between widely different pitches.

Opinions differ on how well infants can localize sound—that is, tell where the sound is coming from. Many experts have stated that this ability does not develop for several months. However, some recent reports note the ability to locate sounds much earlier. Newborns are said to turn their head to the spoken word, and one baby who was studied when he was only a few minutes old, followed with his eyes the direction of a moving click of sound.

Possibly the most amazing demonstration of an infant's ability to respond to sound is shown in a film depicting newborns' abilities (produced at Case Western University by Dr. Maureen Hack). While an adult talked to an infant only a few days old, Dr. Hack filmed the baby's reactions. The baby actually moved in rhythm to the pitch and pace of the adult's words. Seen in slow motion, the baby's arms and legs flexed and moved as in a ballet, synchronized to the "music" and rhythm of the spoken word. This amazing interaction, it is theorized, is possibly preparing the baby for later language development.

Touch, Smell, and Taste. Less work has been done on these three senses because they don't play as large a role in a baby's early life and development. But it is clear that these senses are also present and working at birth. Newborns, and even fetuses, are sensitive to both pressure and touch. Newborns have been shown to respond to a disagreeable odor, which demonstrates that they can smell. And by changes in their sucking behavior, they have indicated that they can taste the differences between water, acidic liquids, sugar, salt solutions, and milk.

Advanced Behaviors

We now know that babies enter the world with all five senses in working order. Even more amazing than this finding are the results of studies showing very young infants capable of even more complex behaviors—behaviors that require some sort of mental processing of the information received through their senses.

For example, infants as young as two months will follow the gaze of an adult to look where the adult is looking. This use of another person as a guide is a much more advanced skill than just looking at the other person and indicates a baby's quickly expanding ability to interact with his environment.

At a very young age, babies also show purposeful cause-and-effect behavior, according to Jerome S. Bruner of Harvard University, a leading researcher in infant development. He devised an apparatus that brings a motion picture into focus when a baby sucks on a pacifier at a prescribed rate (one suck per second). Six-week-old infants learned to suck at exactly the right speed to keep the picture in focus. To do this, they had to coordinate these two ordinarily unrelated activities of sucking and looking.

Another advanced skill—and one of the biggest surprises in this research —is how quickly a baby hears the differences in voices. It has been shown that by three weeks of age, babies react differently to their mother's, father's, or a stranger's voice. When a baby heard her father's voice behind her, her eyes widened and her face lit up eagerly. The baby expected to be played with and tousled by her father. When the baby heard her mother's voice, she had a more composed, waiting look on her face, as if she anticipated being changed, fed, or talked to quietly. The baby listened to the stranger's voice without much reaction except for a slightly apprehensive look on her face.

Dr. Michael Lewis, a senior research psychologist at Educational Testing Service's Institute for Research Development, states that, very young, "An infant can recognize and respond to his mother's voice and face, connecting them at perhaps as early as one month old. By 12 weeks a baby can tell whether his mother is talking to him or to someone else." When Dr. Lewis showed a baby his mother's face behind soundproof glass but piped in a stranger's voice from a microphone in front of the mother's mouth, "The infant looked around as if trying to figure out what was wrong." That young baby was too smart to be fooled.

An astonishing achievement for newborns was reported in late 1977 by two psychologists at the University of Washington in Seattle. Andrew N. Meltzoff and M. Keith Moore discovered that infants just 12 to 21 days old could imitate facial and manual gestures. One of the researchers systematically made faces at 18 infants—sticking out his tongue, opening his mouth, or pursing his lips. He also opened and closed his hand. The babies reacted by imitating all four gestures.

Traditionally the ability to mimic facial expressions has been considered a milestone in infant development and wasn't thought to be possible until about eight to twelve months of age because it involves a combined perceptual/cognitive process: matching a gesture a baby sees with a gesture of his own which he cannot see.

Alertness And Attention

Of course, new babies do not spend all day looking, listening, and learning. A baby's attentiveness varies considerably, depending on his level of arousal. Based on some unique observations of newborns, Dr. Peter Wolf recognized six distinctly different ways of being in the world.

Of the three alert states—quiet alert, active alert, and crying—the first is immensely important for learning. The infant is quiet but attentive. He focuses on visual objects and follows their movement, orients to sounds, and responds to social stimuli like faces, voices, cuddling, and holding. Newborns during their first week spend only ten percent of their day in this quiet alert state, but this percentage soon increases.

In the other two awake states, infants are less attentive. In the active alert state, the baby's arms and legs flex energetically, and his eyes rove aimlessly without focusing on objects. During crying, attentiveness disappears, but it is possible to induce the state of attention again by picking up the baby on one's shoulders and soothing him. Thus mothers who pick up their crying babies give them more opportunities to be visually alert and scan their environment.

Besides these internally determined levels of arousal, an external factor commonly affects an infant's alertness at birth, according to pediatrician Dr. T. Berry Brazelton of Boston. Brazelton, noted for his research in infant alertness, and others have found that mothers who receive heavy medication during labor have babies who look less at their surroundings. The more drugs given the mother, and the closer to delivery, the less attentive the infant. The depressant effect on the baby lasts at least four days.

Raising Alert Babies

Future research will tell us more about exactly how babies learn. We do know in general that early experience can affect development.

Parents can foster their baby's development by talking and playing with him, cuddling him, and just generally interacting with him. Responding to the baby with lots of personal contact gives him opportunities to learn about himself, others, and his surroundings. For example, parents' facial expressions can help babies learn about appropriate emotional responses.

Social interaction is an important part of an infant's perceptual environment right from birth. For instance, Dr. Kenneth S. Robson at the National Institute of Mental Health has found that eye-to-eye contact between mothers and infants is important to the babies' development, adding to their later attraction to faces and lack of fear of strangers.

Since a baby's motor development at first lags far behind his sensory and perceptual abilities, he can't maneuver to discover and explore new things without his parents' help. Keeping him near people when he is awake and offering plenty of bright, attractive things for him to look at, provides a good learning environment. Researchers think that infants who are kept in a stimulating environment tend to be particularly alert. Even in his crib, the baby won't be bored if the parent uses brightly colored sheets or patterned crib bumpers, and hangs colorful mobiles or other interesting objects overhead for him to practice focusing on.

Earlier assumptions that newborns couldn't do anything except eat, sleep, and cry are now being proved wrong by researchers. Right from birth the infant is working at devloping the skills and information he needs to deal with the world around him. The more we can interact with him and provide him with opportunities for learning, the more we can help him in this important task.

The R-Rated Picture Book

by Tunie Munson

Children's literature specialist Tunie Munson talks about the powerful influence that picture books can have on a young child's sex role development.

She is settled in my lap, and we are gently rocking. Reverently, I open the book. Once again, I will woo my daughter to sleep with vivid words and images. I will bring the imprint of immortal rhymes to her dreams. Go to sleep, my child, as the message echoes in your ears.

I begin to read:

"A woman, a spaniel and a walnut tree; the more you beat them the better they be."

Here it is, waiting in ambush, in the pages of Marguerite de Angeli's delicately wrought *Book of Nursery and Mother Goose Rhymes*. Here it is, with Peter Pumpkin Eater, who incarcerated his first wife and, until he became literate, refused to love his second. Here it is with Polly Flinders, whipped by her mother for spoiling her ''nice new clothes'' in an attempt to warm her little toes. Pages away are cowardly Miss Muffett and Sulky Sue, who is ordered to face the wall until she can produce a smile. And there is the old-woman-who-lived-in-a-shoe and beats her children for lack of a better idea of what to do with them.

I stop, mid-sentence, unable to go on. I sit with my child, destined, I hope, to become what she wants to be. It's a new era, I tell myself, when male or female will be treated as human being, not as stereotype. That hope pushes me past the offending verse and past others like:

"Needles and pins, needles and pins, when a man marries, his trouble begins."

The peace of the moment shattered, I search the pages for the benign ''Hey Diddle Diddle'' or ''Wee Willie Winkie.'' And I wonder how many other babies will hear these rhymes and their messages and assimilate them for life.

Once I laughed at those who could find in the most innocuous tales material worthy of censure or who could read sin and sex into the simplest stories. But I'm no longer laughing. Now, as a parent, I see sexism in many simple children's stories. And I am not alone. Authorities have discovered damaging stereotypes that are presented to children at a time when they are actively determining their own sex roles.

By the time they reach kindergarten, children have identified the appropriate behavior for boys and girls, men and women. Many of their ideas come from picture books, which have persuasive power, and children accept the values in these books.

As one group of researchers noted: "Rigid sex-role definitions not only foster unhappiness in children, but they also hamper the child's fullest intellectual and social development."

Yet, in 1980, the majority of children's picture books still fail to offer a balanced picture of male and female options. The female character has been practically nonexistent, though girls and women comprise 51 percent of the population. In the last five decades, the number of females in children's books has steadily declined.

In one study, for example, researchers found a ratio of 11 males to one female in recent Caldecott award-winning picture books (presented annually by the Children's Service Committee of the American Library Association). The ratio of male to female animal characters was 95 to one.

In much of children's literature, boys are depicted as being active, and girls are passive. Consider, for example, Richard Scarry's "Things We Do," part of his popular *Best Word Book Ever.* Out of 35 figures actively shouting, jumping, drawing, falling, building—only two are females. And what do these two creatures do? One "sits," the other "watches."

It is one of the "cult-of-the-apron" books in which women rarely stray from kitchen or vacuum cleaner. My graffiti now grace the pages of this book. I've sketched hair bows on a number of heads to partially correct the imbalance, and I've deleted particularly offensive phrases.

In the majority of books available, the age-old division of labor and loving wins, and the reader loses. Boys forfeit their emotions and learn to resist feeling vulnerable or nurturing or afraid.

And girls usually exist only in relation to males or in a few traditional roles. Women remain only wives and mothers, like the docile mother donkey in *Sylvester And the Magic Pebble;* the harried housefrau in Steven Kellogg's *Can I Keep Him?;* and the timid mom with needlework in hand in the seemingly role-free *Little Fox Goes to the End of the World.*

Despite changes in society and the fact that over 40 percent of women today are in the labor force, the picture book woman is a housebound servant who does tasks that are not too difficult or challenging; and dad rarely shares child care or housework. Illustrations, too, can present distorted images of the sexes. Even in an appealing story seemingly free of stereotypes, children may pick up a different message from the illustrations.

Authors who use the generic ''he'' and ''him'' compound the problem. Educator Alleen Pace Nilsen points out that children interpret language quite literally. ''When they hear such expressions as *chairman*, *brotherly love*, *ten-man team*, and *fellow-man*, they think of men, not the whole human race,'' she says.

As authors Miller and Swift of *Words and Women* suggest: ''Younger children have no way of knowing that the mouse or the turtle or the crocodile referred to as *he* is not necessarily a male.'' Authorities like child psychologist Dr. Lee Salk and pediatrician Dr. Benjamin Spock recognize the harm done by such language. They can see, as Spock puts it, ''the ultimately damaging effects of using the pronouns he and him exclusively.''

Clearly, the problem exists, but what is a parent to do about it? To begin with, parents can meet the challenge of identifying sexist content in the children's books they already own. At our house we occasionally edit such language, with no damage done to the flow or style of the prose. We've found that even non-sexist books may contain a passage that is confusing to the preschool listener.

In *Noisy Nancy Norris*, a book recommended for its active heroine, we changed ''When she was a garbage man'' to ''When she was a garbage collector.'' We've penciled in ''fire fighter'' (in a book about a girl hoping to become a fire *man)* and switched policeman to ''police officer'' in another.

When our daughter wondered aloud how her pediatrician could manage to be both a doctor and a woman, we talked about her impressions. Not only had two friends insisted that women could only be nurses, but also none of the books or TV shows she'd seen had featured a female doctor. We then introduced her to Harlow Rockwell's *My Doctor* and Gunilla Wolde's *Tommy Goes To The Doctor,* both excellent books in which the doctor happens to be a woman. This evidence seemed to allay any fears that her pediatrician was an impostor.

Likewise, parents can ensure that among all the books from library and bookstore, the role-free children's book finds a place. Certain stores specialize in a category of books free of stereotypes. At least two of these—Learn Me (642 Grand Avenue, St. Paul, MN 55105) and The Children's Book and Music Center (5373 W. Pico Boulevard, Los Angeles, CA 90019)—will send a free catalog on request. An excellent bibliography dealing specifically with nonstereotyped picture books is "Books For Today's Children," a list of 200 examples compiled in 1979 by Jeanne Bracken and Sharon Wigutoff. (It's available from Learn Me and from The Feminist Press in Old Westbury, N.Y.)

We cannot underestimate the impact of a single reading from a recommended book. In March of 1978, Gary and Linda Berg-Cross reported some amazing findings in *The Reading Teacher*. They discovered that the expressed attitudes and values of four- to six-year-old children could be significantly changed by merely hearing a picture storybook once. Storybooks read to the children espoused attitudes and values truly different from those they held. For example, pretest scores supported the finding that children are highly aware of stereotypic sex roles by age four. However, the effect of counter-information, as presented in one of the books, *William's Doll* by Charlotte Zolotow, seemed powerful enough to change a good part of the child's expressed values.

This study revealed the dramatic influence that books can have on preschool children. And it suggests that parents and teachers should take more seriously the books they introduce to children.

Aware of this discovery, I instituted a weekly storytime at our four-year-old's nursery school. With the cooperation of the staff, I was able to introduce stories that affirmed all kinds of experiences and lifestyles. I then sent notes briefly describing these stories to parents so they could share the same books—borrowed or bought—with their children at home.

Often a related activity reinforced the story's theme. One morning we shared Charlotte Pomerantz' irresistible ode to spring—*The Piggy in the Puddle*. In the tale sister pig affirms the value of "squishy-squashy, mooshy-squooshy, oofy-poofy" mud and ignores her family's barbs about messiness, until each member succumbs to the lure of a good "wallow."

After the story, we cooked up a "Sandbox Sandwich," "Backyard Stew" and "Pine Needle Upside Down Cake" (from *Mudpies and Other Recipes* by Marjorie Winslow). The cooks—including two girls who initially worried about getting dirty and a boy who eschewed "cooking"—accepted the invitation to help out. Many created their own mudpies at home.

But stories themselves have an inherent attraction. *George The Babysitter* is an example. It tells about a caregiver who "sits" when Mother goes to work. Of author-illustrator Shirley Hughes' delightful story, one critic wrote, "The best picture book yet about a modern family" and another reviewer termed it a "blissfully real and happy book for toddlers."

The children at school obviously agreed. They enjoyed studying the detailed illustrations. (So do many parents who recognize in the cluttered kitchen and bedroom a closer approximation to reality than in most books depicting the perfectly tidy home.)

Contributing a list of recommended stories or finding nonsexist library books to supplement a school collection does make a difference. But charity begins at home, and the expenditure of money or time need not be great. A range of inexpensive paperbacks exists for those who wish to augment a collection. Affordable hardcovers exist as well. Gunilla Wolde's series of Betsy books *(Betsy's Fixing Day, Betsy's Baby Brother)* has an honored place on our shelves and in our hearts. And Betsy's counterpart, Tommy, figures in another series by Wolde.

Books like Astrid Lindgren's *Of Course Polly Can Ride A Bike* or Patricia Lee Lauch's *Christina Katerina And The Box* disprove the old notion that boys won't show an interest in books about girls. Polly, Christina Katerina, and others like them are exciting, resourceful characters with whom any child readily identifies. Similarly, mind- (and role-) expanding books like Arnold Adoff's *Make A Circle Keep Us In* (featuring a nurturing, cuddly dad) and Joe Lasker's *Mothers Can Do Anything* (providing a profile of women in diverse activities) deserve to be included in a regular family storytime.

By becoming discriminating readers (and viewers of illustrations), we protect our children's right to realize their full potential. By offering alternatives in the pages of their books, we affirm the drive to develop, as experts suggest, into whole persons.

No parents can guarantee that their offspring will live happily ever after. But as our children begin life's journey, we can, with love and support, bring them books that show the myriad roads they can follow.

Dyslexia: More Common Than It Sounds

by Vella C. Munn

"I sas tha be r defor klaz." A clever puzzle? No. The writing of a young boy with dyslexia. But now there are ways to help cure this reading disability.

Your perfect baby is doing everything according to schedule. As you watch your child reaching out to playmates, learning how to handle a ball, putting on the right shoe, his happy chatter and intelligent questions reassure you. At least your child won't have trouble in school. Anyone that sure both physically and socially, with a never-ending inquisitiveness, is going to breeze through the school years.

That's what I thought. My son was only four when he started kindergarten, but the teacher and I kept in close contact, and when June rolled around, I felt no qualms about letting him join his classmates in the first grade. Less than a year later, I was in despair. My son hated school. When I listened to him read at home, I couldn't understand why he could be told a word, time and time again, and yet have it remain a mystery the next time he came across it. He frustrated easily, and his teacher told me that he was restless in class. Things got even worse in the second grade. He was in the slow reading class, and because I was doing volunteer work at the school, I knew he was trying hard but without results. I tried to help at home, but I couldn't understand why he persisted in writing letters backwards, had horrible handwriting, and occasionally tried to read from right to left.

Summer was a relief. Maybe he could regain a little of his faltering self-confidence while playing baseball, which he did very well. We'd face the third grade when it came.

As far as I'm concerned, the third grade was the real start of his education. Unknown to me, our school district had embarked on a specific language disability (SLD) program and had hired a teacher, who, in addition to attending a series of workshops on classroom procedure, was now qualified to teach other teachers concerned with the "unreachables" in their classrooms. Under his guidance my son slowly emerged from his depression and began to find joy in the progress he was making. He is now able to keep up with the Yankees in the sports page, which, for him, is what reading is all about.

What Is Dyslexia?

What miracle was that third grade teacher performing? And what is SLD, or dyslexia, as it is often called?

According to Beth Slingerland, head of the Specific Language Disability Slingerland Institute in Seattle, Washington, and developer of the classroom programs for dyslexia most universally used, dyslexia occurs in as much as 30 percent of the population, with the more severe difficulties showing in approximately 10 percent. That means that you as a parent have at least a 10 percent chance of having a child with a learning disability. And if you do, your interest in education will be more intense than other parents'.

A dyslexic is not retarded. This fact can't be stressed enough. The National Advisory Committee on Dyslexia and Related Reading Disorders is quick to point out that Einstein, Leonardo da Vinci, George Washington, and John D. Rockefeller all suffered from dyslexia. But an affected child is fighting an uphill battle in school, especially if that school system doesn't have an active SLD program. Unfortunately, the SLD reading program is taking root slowly in the education system, despite the fact that in the '20s and '30s, Dr. Samuel Orton, a neuropsychiatrist and neuropathologist, identified the syndrome of developmental reading disability and separated it from mental defect and brain damage. In the early '30s Dr. Orton and Anna Gillingham devised a one-to-one teaching technique that was subsequently revised by Mrs. Slingerland for use in normal classroom settings. But as recently as 1974, only Boston, parts of Washington, California, and Texas were holding summer schools to educate teachers in the specific techniques needed to reach SLD children.

Educating educators in the special needs of dyslexics is catching on. But even if SLD reading programs become as commonplace as teaching the multiplication tables, it doesn't release us as parents from the need to learn all we can about what causes a bright child to burst into tears at the sight of a written page.

The Dyslexic Child

What is a dyslexic child? This isn't an easy question to answer since each child reacts in an individual way. Some neurologists believe that dyslexia is caused by a confusion in brain function. In the dyslexic it is suggested that both halves of the brain may be trying to do the same work. Dr. Laurelle Bender, developer of the Bender Visual-Motor Gestalt Test, holds the theory that a difference in the maturation of the functional areas of the brain and personality is responsible for the child who doesn't fit the mold. The Orton Society has isolated faulty visual perception in one or more of five parts as being at the root of the child's problem. But whatever the cause, the real question is how to treat the problem.

The dyslexic child is of average or above-average intelligence. He or she (Mrs. Slingerland has determined that there are four boy dyslexics to every girl) is a child who has trouble learning to read, write, and spell. He may have trouble putting his thoughts into understandable sentences, or he may be highly verbal and have a tendency to dominate the conversation. Dyslexic children contribute well to classroom discussions that deal with general information in social studies, science, and the like. Unless math exercises necessitate problem solving, they often excel in that area. They copy problems from the board incorrectly, "blow" a test in spite of careful study beforehand, put off handing in reports, can't remember directions, and quit before completing an assignment.

Early Warning Signs

One of the most frustrating aspects of dyslexia is that it seldom surfaces before a child reaches school age—the age at which he has to contend with letters that scramble themselves or have a tendency to wander within a word, and be able to tell left from right. But now that I've gone through the experience with my son, I see that there were some early signs, even if I didn't know it then. The Orton Society's research shows that dyslexia tends to run in families, with fathers usually passing the disability on to their sons. But I have horrible handwriting, throw up my hands at math, and can't spell—all of which tend to label me as dyslexic myself. In other words, if you or other relatives say, "Oh, I never could spell and no one can read my handwriting," the warning light should go on. This doesn't necessarily mean that the children of all poor readers are dyslexic, but if in addition, your preschooler can't remember to put on his socks, comb his hair, and get into the car without having each request repeated separately, you will probably want to watch his first few years of school closely and start asking questions if he has trouble keeping up with the class, despite average or above-average intelligence.

Other early signs that may, but not necessarily, point to dyslexia have been isolated by Mrs. Slingerland. They include persistently reversing letters and numbers; working from right to left; having trouble with verbal expression; showing a lack of good, clear hand preference; doing messy work; showing poor small muscle control; and accomplishing work slowly or not at all. A child who uses brief phrases or words to express himself, enunciates poorly, can't articulate clearly, and can't always repeat a word after hearing, may be trying to tell us something.

The World Federation of Neurology identifies dyslexia as a disorder in children who, despite conventional classroom experience, fail to attain language skills of writing, reading, and spelling commensurate with their intellectual abilities. Although this definition puts pressure on the schools to find an alternate means of reaching those children, it doesn't do much to help us parents. When our children hurt, we hurt. We want and need to know what the problem is and what we can do to help. Our system of education has conditioned most of us to leave the teaching of reading, writing, and spelling skills to teachers. But the child who is failing at school is the same child who comes home carrying that feeling of failure with him. The embarrassment and frustration experienced at school and play will be reflected in his behavior at home.

How Parents Can Help

The best way to take pressure off a dyslexic child is to find out as much as possible about his problems. It isn't the child's fault that he can't remember to do what he's told. Angry parents only reinforce his feelings that he's no good. Instead of anger, he desperately needs understanding. We can help by reading homework assignments aloud, helping him talk through the thought problems in math, and helping him get them written down. A dyslexic child doesn't want his work done for him, but he can't be sent off by himself to do it. He needs help in checking his work to make sure it is correct. When it comes to giving him chores to do around the house, we should give simple directions, in short sentences, and not too many at a time. If he needs to be corrected, it should be done quietly and not in front of the whole family.

What, ideally, is the school doing at the same time? I was invited to sit in on several sessions and watch the entire class write letters in the air, which, in addition to imprinting the letter formation in the mind, also utilizes body movement to increase coordination. I learned that dyslexic children confuse the smallest units of sight and sound so that letters such as *b-d, u-n, w-m, p-g* refuse to remain separate from one another. To counter this, children are taught to associate sight and sound symbols with the "feel" of these symbols. Saying a letter out loud while writing it in the air was one means Orton-Gillingham and then Mrs. Slingerland used to help the child get a letter and subsequently words and whole sentences to "behave themselves" in a child's mind.

Getting educators to recognize and then help dyslexics will become nationwide only when parents demand such programs. Testing for dyslexia can be requested on an individual basis if the school doesn't do it as a matter of course, but that's only the first step. I remember seeing the writing of a twelve-year-old, which came out something like this: "I sas tha be r defor klaz." This boy had an IQ of 130, but his written message was gibberish to everyone including himself. I am thankful that my son won't have to experience this boy's intense frustration. And with widespread parental and educator knowledge, today's children hopefully won't have their initial enthusiasm for school shattered in a few years.

Dyslexia isn't a disease or something to be ashamed of. It is a specific language disability that can be handled in a normal classroom through the joint effort of trained teachers and concerned parents.

Is TV Bad For Your Child?
by Pamela C. Smith

Here are some of the experts' answers to this question plus suggestions on how you can enhance your child's TV viewing.

When Marianne and Brad discussed their plans for raising a family, they vowed never to let their children watch too much television. "I might let them watch *Sesame Street,*" Brad said, "but as far as commercial TV goes, there's just too much violence."

"Not to mention the junk food commercials," Marianne added. "No wonder mothers have trouble getting their kids to eat right."

Deena, mother of two preschoolers and pregnant with her third, is also concerned about the influence of television. "It's amazing how much the kids pick up from TV," she said. "Even my eighteen-month-old can sing the jingles from the commercials she sees. It bothers me that the 'idiot box' may be socializing my kids as much as I am."

Electronic Baby-Sitter

As the controversy over the effects of television on children ignites the airwaves, young parents are voicing concern. Yet, in spite of a growing public awareness of the potential dangers of TV, studies show that preschoolers are spending more time staring at the video screen than ever. At the Yale University Family Television Research and Consultation Center, Dr. Dorothy Singer and her colleagues have discovered that most 2-1/2 to 4-year-olds watch from three to four hours of television a day.

The TV set has become an integral part of the American home. And as most parents of toddlers soon discover, this luminous, inanimate object that spews forth a fast-paced mélange of sight and sound is capable of capturing the attention of an unruly urchin for hours. The problem is apparent: it is all too easy to let TV become a kind of electronic baby-sitter for our children. As Deena explains: "I welcome the Saturday morning cartoon-fest because I know it will keep the girls out of my hair for a few hours so I can get my housework done."

While this attitude is understandable, it is undeniably dangerous to let children watch too much unsupervised TV.

Violence and Aggression

The most widely publicized reason for limiting TV viewing is the amount of violence on the airwaves. Dr. George Gerbner of the University of Pennsylvania's Annenberg School of Communications, who devised the Television Violence Profile, recently reported an increase in the number of violent incidents shown during Saturday morning cartoon programming.

Many researchers have found a definite link between preschoolers' aggressive behavior and the amount of TV violence they are exposed to. At Yale Dr. Singer reports that preschoolers who are heavy viewers of action-adventure shows—including cartoons—are more physically aggressive than other children. (According to the Yale researchers, physical aggression means actual physical violence, such as one child hitting another, and destruction of property. Their definition does not include unintentional aggressiveness during play or make-believe activities.)

Children learn through imitation, and they will imitate the aggressive behavior they see on the screen. They may also learn anti-social *values* from TV and begin to believe that violence is the best way to resolve conflicts.

Excessive viewing of TV violence can also have a damaging emotional effect on young children. According to Dr. Isidore Ziferstein, a leading child psychiatrist and member of the board of directors of the National Association for Better Broadcasting, five- and six-year-olds who were studied showed an increase in nightmares, fears, and disturbed sleep and appetites. One reason for the anxiety that some children display after viewing violent or frightening program content is that they are unable to discriminate fantasy from reality. Many children become upset and confused because to them, TV is the real world. They may not like what they view and feel unable to control it.

The "Gimme Syndrome"

Violence is only part of the picture. Citizen's groups like Action for Children's Television have rallied against the amount of commercial messages for children. Several years ago they pressured the National Association of Broadcasters (NAB) to adopt guidelines that reduced the amount of commercial time on children's programs. Now they are proposing that the Federal Trade Commission (FTC) ban *all* commercials directed at children, using the regulation that outlaws deceptive advertising.

Since studies have shown that preschoolers do not understand the persuasive or "selling" content of commercials and that very young children cannot even discriminate between the advertisements and the programs, ACT and other groups of concerned parents and educators feel that advertising geared to children is indeed "deceptive." Any parent who has heard "Mommy, buy me that" and other pleas characteristic of the "gimme syndrome," would probably welcome such a ban. But network officials are quick to point out that commercial television is big business, and ads hawking cereals and toys pay the bills. Often the profits from commercials aired on low-budget, Saturday morning cartoon programs are what finance quality children's programming—like CBS's *Captain Kangaroo,* and for older children, NBC's *Special Treat* and ABC's *After-School Specials.*

The Positive Side

These programs represent the positive side of television for children. Even on the networks, there are a few bright oases in the desert wasteland of children's TV. Several of these thoughtful, imaginative new programs, including *Carra-scolendas* and *Villa Alegre* for preschoolers, are government-funded and independently produced. Nate Long, executive director of TVaC (Television for All Children), which produced these and other award-winning, child-oriented series, explains that network affiliates are beginning to seek out these shows.

Public TV, free of advertisements, still airs superior children's fare. *Mister Rogers' Neighborhood,* with a low-key, slow-paced approach, is a favorite of many preschoolers. Dr. Singer and her colleagues at Yale have found that children who are heavy viewers of *Mister Rogers* are less aggressive, more cooperative and imaginative than children who get large doses of action, cartoon, and game shows.

Sesame Street, the most widely researched, written-about, and highly-praised children's show ever, is still going strong as it enters its eleventh season. Research has proven its effectiveness in teaching pre-language and pre-math skills that help ready the preschooler for kindergarten. *Sesame Street* also provides role models for disadvantaged children and teaches preschoolers such pro-social behavior as cooperation and sharing.

But even an intelligent, entertaining show like *Sesame Street* has more positive impact on a child when the parents encourage him to watch it, view the show with him, and discuss aspects of the program later on. This is the one basic principle with regard to children and television on which child psychologists, educators, media experts, and network officials all agree: the role of the parent is crucial.

Parents' Responsibility

Dr. Edward L. Palmer, director of research at Children's Television Workshop (which produces *Sesame Street*), recently expressed his concern over parents who use television as a baby-sitter. He stressed the importance of parents' setting limits on the amount of television their children watch and suggested ways that parents can enhance the positive aspects of the viewing experience.

"Watch with the children from time to time," Dr. Palmer recommends. "Be aware of everything they watch, and be familiar with the content and quality. Take the time to log a week of the TV your child views. By writing it down, you may see more clearly the need to restrict certain programs."

Dr. Palmer suggests that parents contact their local ACT group to get recommendations about suitable programs. The National Education Association and the NABB also have program endorsement listings.

"Read through the TV guide each week and make it a point to note when educational, interesting programs will be aired," Dr. Palmer advises. "Watch for children's specials, particularly around holiday times.

"Sit and discuss the program with the child. Find out what he liked and didn't like. Ask questions; probe. Have him tell you what he thought the program was about. Discuss the nature of television; try to make sure the child understands what is real and what is fantasy."

TVaC's executive director, Nate Long, offers these suggestions:

"Parents must speak up. They've got to let the broadcasters know what they want for their kids. Write letters to the local affiliates, barrage the Federal Communications Commission (the government regulatory agent that oversees the broadcasting industry) with complaints. Too many people don't even realize that the FCC licenses stations to serve the public. They don't realize that if they call and complain, by law, their call will be logged. The public must be educated, and they must be made aware that they do have a voice in what comes on the screen. Parents have a responsibility to fight for better children's programming."

While there is debate over the amount of responsibility the government and the industry should take for children's programming, one thing is clear: parents have the most immediate impact on how television will affect their kids.

When Your Child Stutters

by Candace Moon

"Listen! He's talking!" How many parents have shouted this phrase proudly upon hearing their toddler say his first word? Listening to a baby's cooing and gurgling turn into actual words is always exciting. When my three-year-old daughter, Donna, first began communicating with words, I was like most parents.

"She's talking now," I would announce proudly to friends, neighbors, and relatives. And to Donna I would coax, "Say mama."

But like most parents, I paid less attention to my child's utterances as she developed new skills such as dressing herself and learning how to eat without dumping the plate over her head. Her vocabulary grew by leaps and bounds, and I took her verbal expressions for granted.

Until a few months ago. She simply awoke one day with her normal verbal fluency gone.

"M-m-m-m-m-m," she struggled miserably.

"M-m-m-m-mom-e-e-e-e-"

I immediately stopped pouring the milk over her cereal and looked at my daughter in astonishment as she sat perched at the kitchen table. Trying to address me, her eyes were closed and her small head nodded with the effort.

"B-b-b-b-b-break-f-f-f-fast."

The next few days were like a nightmare. Used to my child's nonstop talking, I was thrown entirely off balance. I tried everything. Later I was to learn that I probably compounded the problem by my reactions to her stuttering, but at the time, I felt frantic enough to try any approach that happened to pop into my head. I tried ignoring it and instead ignored *her.* I tried treating it with light humor but abandoned that idea when I realized I was inadvertently encouraging her to laugh at other people's speech defects. As I became more upset over the situation, I became more and more impatient with my daughter. And the stuttering just became worse.

The third day after the stuttering appeared, I decided to call the family doctor for advice. It was then that Donna unexpectedly pointed to a scar on her cheek and began a frustrated attempt to talk.

"D-d-d-d-d-d-dog d-d-d-d-did th-th-th-th-th-th-at. D-d-d-d-d-donna h-h-h-h-h-hurt."

Then everything seemed to fall into place. The previous winter she had been attacked by a dog, and the severity of the injuries required that she be rushed to the hospital for several stitches. At the time she took it surprisingly well, never complaining throughout the whole unpleasant ordeal. In fact several people remarked on how little she had been affected by it, and not wanting to remind her of the unpleasant experience, I never referred to it. But now, taking her little gesture to her face as a cue, I decided to talk about it—how the dog had bitten her, how the nice doctor "made it all better," how much Mommy and Daddy loved her.

And the next morning I had my little girl back. Almost as dramatically as the stuttering appeared, it disappeared. But I have noticed that occasionally, when I am hurried and not giving her the usual amount of attention, she tends to stutter. Although the worst of the problem certainly appears to be over, the experience did raise several questions, especially about the conflicting advice I got from friends and relatives.

Just what causes a child to stutter?

"Actually no one knows the real reason that people stutter," says Dr. Lloyd Augustine at the University of Oregon Speech Pathology Department. "We have studied it for years and years and nobody yet knows the cause of it." The problem is old enough to have been referred to in ancient Egyptian tablets, and it has been suspected that Moses was afflicted with it. It affects almost five times as many males as females. And it is still a mystery.

Over the years, however, a few theories have evolved from the study of the problem. Some speech therapists feel that stuttering is the result of a shock or a mental conflict. Although this theory seems to explain my daughter's sudden stuttering, many children who have never suffered a trauma have developed a stuttering problem. Also many children who have survived very frightening ordeals never stutter afterwards, causing other speech pathologists to believe the disorder is neurologically latent and surfaces because of environmental conditions.

The most widely accepted theory at this time suggests that when parents react to normal nonfluencies (repetitions, backtracking, blocks, or pauses) as if it were stuttering, the child will usually stutter more.

"Parents should be aware that in children there are normal nonfluencies," Dr. Augustine warns. "And sometimes parents interpret these *normal* nonfluencies as being *abnormal*. And so they start working on the child. One theory, by Wendell Johnson, is that stuttering begins in the listener's ear. The parent hears the child making these normal nonfluencies and reacts to them in an abnormal way. The child desires to correct these normal nonfluencies, and in the process of trying to correct them, the problem gets worse. The worse it becomes the more he tries. It's a vicious cycle."

Experts in the field of speech pathology have noticed that children who stutter are generally more tense than other children. But in keeping with the mysterious nature of stuttering, no one really knows for sure if the tension is the cause or the effect of the disorder. It's like the proverbial question about the chicken or the egg.

Despite disagreement among speech pathologists about the actual cause or causes of stuttering, all agree that the environment in which a child develops his speech plays an important role.

"Stuttering is a social interaction problem," comments Dr. Augustine. "Most of the time stutterers don't have a chance to talk. We try to get parents to reduce the pressures in the home. We can take people in our clinic and get them into an acceptable environment where they know that *we* know what their problem is. And after a while they are highly fluent. They talk very fluently because we don't try to interrupt or judge them. But they walk out of the door and the problem comes back. One of the most difficult things for a speech therapist is the breakdown when the client leaves the clinical setup."

How can parents tell the difference between normal nonfluencies and stuttering? Although it would be difficult to count the actual number of times your child speaks with repetitions, there are about fifty nonfluencies for each one thousand words spoken in normal speech.

"If the child says, 'I want-want-want,' that's really not a danger sign," continues the therapist. "But when he starts stuttering on syllables—'I wa-wa-wa-want,' or prolongations, 'I waaaaaaaaaant,' the parent should be concerned. Also if the child asks, 'Why can't I talk right?' or if he shows some frustration in his speaking, this is a cause for concern. Or if anyone in the child's environment identifies it as stuttering, then the child should be evaluated."

Some of the things I tried with Donna were mentioned as common but damaging mistakes a parent can make.

"Telling a child to stop and start over is deadly poison to a stutterer," cautions

Dr. Augustine, "or telling him to think before he speaks. *We all* think before we speak."

It's easy to take our children's speech for granted, yet it is one of the most valuable abilities that they have. The following advice for parents is offered by experts, not only for parents of children who stutter, but for all parents who want to help their children develop good speech.

1. Don't call attention to your child's nonfluencies, especially by telling him to stop or start over. You might want to enlist the cooperation of people who often come in contact with your child such as teachers, relatives, and baby-sitters.

2. We all know children look to us as examples. Do you talk in a relaxed way? As busy homemakers, it's easy to adopt a rushed and hurried way of speaking, and this can easily convince a child that words should be spoken as rapidly as possible.

3. "When he speaks, look the child in the eye," Dr. Augustine suggests. And wait until he gets it out. Many times little children get excited and can't get it out because they don't have the neuro-muscular control over the articulators. It's just that the nervous system is all geared up, and that's the time you really have to be patient with him."

4. Let your child know he'll get his chance to be heard. Stuttering often appears in active families where the children feel they have to compete verbally for parental attention. Setting aside a certain time each day just to listen is a great way to convince your child you are really interested in what he has to say. And it can also set a pattern that will keep the lines of communication open as your child reaches the teen-age years.

5. Don't interfere with your child's natural hand preference.

6. Family sing-alongs and activities relying on the use of speech (puppets, story-telling) are fun and can also help your child learn to associate talking with pleasurable experiences.

7. Just like almost everything else, good speech is related to good health. Keep in mind that fatigue and overexcitement will often have an adverse effect on the way your child communicates verbally.

8. If you notice what you think is a stuttering problem, have your child evaluated by a qualified professional. If the child is not yet in school, ask your family doctor to refer you to a speech therapist.

The Nightmares Of Childhood
by Henry Weil

What causes the horrors of the dark and what parents can do about them.

Justin was having nightmares, sometimes two or three a night. They came in waves, some of which lasted for weeks. His mother and I were worried. Some of his dreams made no sense to us at all. ("A witch was trying to make a shirt out of me.") Dr. Spock was no help. So far as we could learn from *Baby and Child Care,* children should have no more nightmares than adults. So we went to see the headmistress of his nursery school.

"Oh yes," she soothed, "it's perfectly normal. All children go through this between the ages of three and six. I'd be worried if Justin *weren't* having night-mares." Could this be true? We checked with our friends. Sure enough, Noah was terrified by scarecrows that settled into his crib and refused to budge. Sarah was upset about the lion and tiger that glared in at her bedroom window at the same moment a large crack ripped through her bedroom wall. Christopher dreamed he was in a strange house with one very dark room in which a small, unidentifiable object glowed and said to him, "Better leave and not come back, because if you do, you'll never leave again." Panic, screams, tears.

What did all this mean? Few adults, it turns out, remember their late-night agonies or indeed much else that happened to them between the ages of three and six. Consequently, some parents are unprepared, as we were, when lengthy bouts of nightmares strike their children. Surprisingly, when I tried to learn what is known about children's nightmares, I discovered that they have been less thoroughly researched than other areas in child psychology.

Freud, who considered adult dreams the royal road to the unconscious, casually dismissed children's dreams as undisguised wish-fulfillment and not very inter-esting. Decades passed before Freud's clinical heirs discovered that children's dreams are often prompted less by wish-fulfillment than by agonizing guilt, and that what children fear, rationally or irrationally, during the day can return to plague them at night.

Studying Children's Dreams

There are obvious difficulties researching children's dreams. First, we all know how quickly the memory of most dreams crumbles and fades. Then, too, young-sters have limited vocabularies with which to describe their dreams, and they quickly become self-conscious and reticent if they feel their experiences are belittled or distorted. Finally, since children easily trot out waking fantasies simply playing with toys or pretending, children's analysts seldom need to use dreams as an entry to a child's subconscious. Consequently, few careful studies of children's dreams have made their way into medical literature.

But we do know a few things. "The first definite proof of dreams in children we have observed," wrote world-famous child psychologist Jean Piaget, "came between the age of 21 months and 2 years, when the children talked in their sleep and gave an account of dreams when they awoke." But infants less than a year old have been observed smiling and even laughing during sleep, and napping newborns are known to produce brain-wave patterns identical to those of dreaming adults. It is probable, therefore, that we all dream from the beginning. No one knows, however, when our dreams first begin to turn sour.

In the late 1940s Dr. J. Louise Despert asked a sampling of nursery-school students what they dreamed about. She was astonished that the children seldom reported happy, playtime dreams but instead repeatedly described "supernatural creatures, mysterious events...physical danger, activities of feared criminals, robbers, kidnappers, and the like, and...misfortune befalling self and others."

Curiously, children who witness someone being seriously injured will probably dream about similar injuries to themselves. But children who have broken a limb, been nearly drowned, or who have experienced a similar disaster, seldom worry about the incident in their sleep. It's as though they have tested the experience, survived it, and no longer need to fear it. What haunts sleeping children, in other words, is the *potential* for injury that they are afraid they can't deal with.

All children, psychologists agree, experience occasional difficulty falling asleep, wake unhappily in the middle of the night, dream of threatening situations (even if the danger seems absurd by the light of day), worry late at night over ghosts, witches, wild animals, and the like, occasionally fear going to sleep alone, want to get into the parents' beds, and sometimes insist on a pre-bedtime ritual. Interestingly, such tendencies often get worse when the child is physically ill. But, experts seem to agree, by themselves these experiences are usually harmless and will only be aggravated into problems if parents believe they are problems and communicate this fear to the child.

Nightmares are often triggered by something that happens to the child the day before. This can be such a harmless event as hearing the roar of a vacuum cleaner, or watching water run down a bathtub drain, or having a doll's arm fall off. One psychologist reports a child who had terrible nightmares after hearing her grandmother say, "Those ants are here again. They will eat *everything* up!"

Another reports a child terrorized by a dream of a blackbird eating the carrot-nose off his snowman's face. His mother had thought she was only making the child laugh when she regularly tweaked his nose and sang, "Along came a blackbird and nipped off her nose."

The Fears Behind Nightmares

The detail that sets off a nightmare is not always the fear the dream is expressing. There are two basic discoveries that all young children make and which they always find frightening. About the time children reach the age of three, they begin to understand that they are separate from the world around them, that mother can go away and not come back the instant she is wanted, and that in the largest sense, they are alone in the world. This thought frightens many people throughout their lives.

Then, about the same time, children also recognize that they have the power to incur disapproval from their parents, to destroy loved toys that are neither mendable nor replaceable, or to fall painfully when they try to climb a bookcase. Not only are they potentially alone in the world, but they are also responsible for painful consequences of their actions. This, too, is a concept some of us wrestle with for years.

The healthy reaction when confronted with these awesome discoveries is to become anxious. Anxiety is the way we anticipate danger so that we can prepare to deal with it. Anxiety over the potential consequences of our independent actions can help us define ourselves, exercise our imaginations and build a socially beneficial conscience. But as anxiety accumulates, it produces nightmares—in adults as well as children.

In confronting our tensions, even in fantasies such as dreams, we find ways of dealing with them, of experiencing them and discovering that we can live through them without serious consequences—in other words, we grow up. One important study of children's nightmares suggested they are "a healthy response to strong provocation or threat."

Is this true, even when nightmares go on night after night for weeks at a time? "It's not a question of duration," explains Dr. Israel Zeifman, child psychiatrist and analyst associated with Mt. Sinai Hospital and the New York Psychoanalytic Institute. "If things are serious, it's more than a single symptom. There's usually a whole pattern of difficulties."

Dr. Esther Mullen, chief psychologist of the Child and Youth Program at Roosevelt Hospital, for instance, advises parents to examine how a child, bothered by nightmares, behaves during the day. If he is fearful and retiring—

or overly aggressive—then he may have a serious problem. But in general, if children seem to be reasonably well adjusted when awake, then their nightmares, grotesque and fearsome as they may sound, are probably reasonably well adjusted too.

Usually, parents can do little more to help children through this painful period than offer comfort and support. If the child demands a pre-bedtime ritual, it may come from a healthy reluctance to abandon this fascinating world even for a few hours, or it may be a mystic defense against the terrors of the night. The reason doesn't matter. If it doesn't go on too long, cooperate. And let the child have toys in bed. They can be precious allies in scaring away hobgoblins.

When children wake in the middle of the night, comfort them, sleepy and half-alert though you are. The younger they are, the more holding they require. In most cases, that's all they'll need. Be careful not to dismiss the object of terror as ridiculous. If someone is utterly convinced there's a witch in the closet, it doesn't help to be told there's no such thing as a witch. (To get the imaginary scarecrows out of Noah's bed, his father had to bawl the scarecrows out, telling them they had no business in Noah's crib and had better not come back.) Whatever the child's fear, be sympathetic. Young children, waking from nightmares, don't understand that dreams aren't really happening and aren't helped by being told they're "only dreaming." Children learn to distinguish dreams from reality slowly over their early years.

If possible, try to figure out which anxiety is bothering the child at the moment and, if you can, ease the pressure during the day. If he or she, for instance, is frightened by dreams of getting dirty, perhaps parents are putting too much pressure on being neat or on toilet training or on something similar. But such detective work is difficult. The younger the child, the harder it is to find the source of anxiety. Infants are rarely able to say more than "chase me," "eat me up," or, least helpful of all, "hold me." Even when children have a sizable vocabulary, they are usually reluctant to experience the terror by talking about it. But don't try psychoanalyzing your child, cautions Dr. Zeifman, especially if you lack clinical training. Parents who do this often end up labeling their child's anxieties (and not always correctly) without getting around to easing them.

The best thing a parent can do in helping a young child cope with nightmares, Dr. Zeifman summarizes, is to "have belief in the kid, confidence in the kid, and acceptance of his anxieties. It's a difficult task."

So what has our increased confidence and acceptance done for Justin? The other night he waked from yet another nightmare, but this was different. "A big puppet was chasing me, saying, 'I love you, I love you,' " he reported. "But that sounds like a nice puppet," I said. "No," Justin assured me, "it was yucky!"

Chapter 4
Health and Safety

How To Save Your Child From Choking
by Jean Caldwell

Three generations of our family like to banish occasional hunger pangs with a nice spoonful of peanut butter straight from the jar. But we're having second thoughts about the practice since Dr. Henry Heimlich said it can be deadly.

Dr. Heimlich is the Cincinnati surgeon whose anti-choking Heimlich Maneuver has saved 3500 lives since 1974. Dr. Heimlich admits that he "loves" peanut butter, but he is concerned that its stickiness puts it in a class by itself when it comes to being a choking hazard. He is aware of two cases where people eating straight peanut butter off the spoon have choked to death. In one instance even a trained emergency room physician working with instruments had great difficulty trying to extract the peanut butter from the lungs of a 54-year-old woman doctor, who later died.

The usual things people choke on—pieces of meat, hard candy, or, in the case of children, small toys—can be dislodged by the Heimlich Maneuver. But peanut butter does its own thing. When someone starts to choke, explains Dr. Heimlich, the instinctive thing they do is cough. But the first step in coughing is to take a breath. Doing this causes the peanut butter to go deeper into the airway, and it can become distributed through the lungs.

"It's somewhat like drowning," notes Dr. Heimlich, "except that in drowning, you have a chance to get the water out with the maneuver. Peanut butter will stick to the walls of the lungs."

Dr. Heimlich believes people should be warned to forego peanut butter straight from the jar and only eat it wrapped in something else, as in a sandwich. In any case, he says, it is important to observe the rules that prevent choking in the first place. Never allow a child to walk or run while eating or to put toys or other non-food items into his mouth. Don't laugh, move about or talk while eating. Cut food into small pieces and chew carefully. If you want an alcoholic beverage, eat first and then drink, because alcohol deadens the palate. Learn how to do the Heimlich Maneuver so that you will be able to save a choking victim.

Dr. Heimlich says that traditional methods of trying to help choking victims by slapping them on the back or trying to remove the offending object with your fingers, can serve to drive things further into the throat. He tried to find a better way after he realized that choking is the sixth leading cause of accidental death in this country. After doing experiments with animals, he realized that the air in the lungs could be used to dislodge whatever was causing the choking. He devised his method with an eye to simplicity.

The first thing to do is to be sure the victim is choking. The best way to find out is to simply ask, "Are you choking?" Often the victim will put a hand to his throat.

Sometimes when people begin to choke at the dinner table, they jump up and run to the bathroom or out of doors. If you see someone do this, follow at once because when breath is cut off, there is only a period of four minutes to restore it before death occurs.

The maneuver itself is easy. If the victim is standing or sitting down, get in back and grasp the victim around the waist. Place your fist, thumbside in, against the soft area above the navel and below the rib cage. Cover your fist with your other hand. Push quickly inward and upward. Repeat until the object is expelled.

The action of your thrust puts pressure on the victim's diaphragm and an "amazing" volume of air rushes from the victim's lungs and pushes the object out.

If the victim is large and the rescuer is small, or if the victim has fallen down, the maneuver can still be performed. In this case be sure the victim is on his back, face up, head straight. Straddle his thighs or hips, facing his head and keeping your knees on the floor. Place the heel of one hand on the soft space below the rib cage and above the navel. Place your other hand on top of the fist and push inward and upward quickly.

In this position you must check the victim's mouth after each thrust because once the object is dislodged, the victim will gasp for air, and this could cause him to choke the object back down. If the first thrust does not dislodge the object, keep repeating the two steps; thrust and check, until the airway is clear.

Dr. Heimlich would like to see the maneuver taught in all schools because he has had so many reports of children using it to save a life.

Take Amy Joan Atkinson of Southfield, Utah.

Amy Joan was four years old when her father, Donald, who is a firefighter, decided to teach the anti-choking maneuver to the older kids in the family who were fifteen, twelve, and eight. Amy Joan just happened to be in the room at the same time.

Some weeks later Amy Joan's mother stepped out of the kitchen while Amy Joan and her two-year-old brother, Dallin, were there. A few minutes later Ann Marie Atkinson came back, and this is what she wrote to Dr. Heimlich: "Dallin was very flushed, with tears running down his cheeks. I thought he must have been crying, but he had a happy look on his face.

"Amy Joan said, 'Dallin was choking. I got behind him and did this, and Dallin blew his food out.' She demonstrated the life-saving motion and pointed to a long, stringy piece of chicken on the table."

Thirteen-year-old Nicholas Renna of West Harrison, New York, came into the kitchen to find that his mother had turned blue and was lying on the floor. Just before she had collapsed from choking on a piece of steak, she had looked at her younger children and thought, "My children are watching. What a terrible thing for them to see me die."

Nicholas did the Heimlich Maneuver, and on the third thrust the steak popped out and Mrs. Renna recovered.

The Krzemienskis of Beaver Falls, Pennsylvania, were on their way home in the car enjoying a snack from a fast food restaurant. Fourteen-year-old Joyce laughed. Seconds later, seventeen-year-old Judy yelled that Joyce was choking and couldn't get her breath. Mrs. Krzemienski later wrote to Dr. Heimlich that she nearly wrecked the car trying to stop in heavy traffic. By the time the car came to a halt, Judy had grabbed her sister and done the Heimlich Maneuver, and the food came loose.

A while back Dr. Heimlich visited Massachusetts to lecture to restaurant workers on his life-saving maneuver. During that single week a father saved the life of his 11-year-old son, who was choking on some popcorn, and another woman saved a diner in a restaurant.

Dr. Heimlich suggests that it would be wiser for a pregnant woman not to participate in demonstrations of the maneuver. But he adds that it should certainly be used on her if she is choking, and she should not hesitate to use it to save someone's life. He reports that actress Goldie Hawn was saved from choking by the Heimlich Maneuver when she was pregnant.

When Should I Call The Doctor?
by Dr. Harris D. Riley, Jr., and Rosemary Welsh

Many new parents are afraid of bothering their pediatrician with unimportant questions about their baby's health. They know that conditions like high or prolonged fever, difficult breathing, and excessive vomiting all demand immediate medical attention. But what about those other conditions that, while certainly not life-threatening, are certainly troublesome. Here are some of the more common things to watch for in your newborn and discuss with your doctor if the need arises.

Jaundice

Two-thirds of full-term infants appear slightly jaundiced on the second or third day of life. By the fourth to seventh day, the yellowish skin color usually disappears. This condition is termed "physiologic jaundice" and is a result of a rise in the serum bilirubin level, which in turn results from the breakdown of fetal red blood cells. Because the liver enzymes aren't mature enough for the first few days after birth to dispose of the spent red blood cells, they build up in the baby's bloodstream. This is indicated by the high bilirubin level. Bilirubin levels of up to 14–15 mg/100 ml are considered acceptable during this period, and no treatment is usually given. But if the levels push higher, your pediatrician will probably recommend that the baby have phototherapy treatments in which his eyes will be covered, and he will be placed under bright lights for several hours each day. This exposure to light helps break down the bilirubin in the bloodstream. A breast-fed baby may also be given formula for a few days to avoid ingesting the hormones in breast milk that inhibit the enzyme responsible for breaking down the bilirubin. In severe cases of jaundice, exchange transfusions may be needed.

Although there are other conditions that may produce jaundice in a newborn, physiologic jaundice is by far the most common in the first week. Later on any yellowish discoloration of the skin or eyeballs should always be reported to your doctor.

Intestinal Disorders

While your baby is in the hospital nursery, the staff will record everything that he consumes as well as every time he wets or soils a diaper. During the first 24 to 36 hours, the staff watches for the passage of meconium, the normal waste product of the early neonatal period that consists of swallowed amniotic fluid, sloughed fetal cells, and digestive juices. The passage of the meconium indicates that the intestine is open and working normally. Next, there is a transition stool that is part meconium and part normal feces. Finally, the normal soft stool appears. Newborns may have a bowel movement every other day or five times a day. Both are normal. The stools of breast-fed infants tend to be yellowish and loose, while those of a bottle-fed infant tend to be darker and better formed.

In the first few hours after birth, vomiting of mucus is not uncommon. Vomiting after the first day of life is usually burping from overfeeding or from failure to sufficiently burp the baby. However, if vomiting from the start persists, your pediatrician will want to rule out malformation of the digestive tract or other disorders.

A newborn can become dehydrated after only a few hours of vomiting. Always consult your doctor if the baby begins to vomit large amounts of fluid after you have come home from the hospital. He will advise you.

Skin Conditions

Are you concerned about small white spots on your baby's face? These spots are called "milia" and are the result of plugged oil glands in the skin. Milia may occur all over the body but are most common on the nose and chin. No treatment is needed, and they disappear by themselves in a few weeks' time.

It's normal for a newborn's skin to look dry and flaky. But after most of these patches have disappeared, scales may be present on the scalp. This condition is called cradle cap and requires vigorous attention. First, clean the scalp twice a day with a cotton ball dipped in baby oil. The oil will soften the crusts so they can be brushed away. If this doesn't work, make a paste of baking soda and water and spread liberally over the scalp. Let it dry for 15 or 20 minutes, then rinse with clear water. Repeat as needed.

Another skin condition requiring prompt attention is impetigo. An outbreak of impetigo may occur in the hospital nursery, but your baby may also develop the infection after coming home. Impetigo is identified by a blister filled with pus and surrounded by a reddened area. The sores may start in the diaper area, in the groin, or under the arm but can also be scattered over the face and arms.

Impetigo is highly contagious, so treatment is mandatory. Once treated, the infection tends to clear up quickly, and the lesions generally don't leave a scar.

Thrush (Oral Monilia)

If you detect a milky coating on the inside of your baby's cheeks that can't be scraped off, the baby may have a yeast infection called thrush. Oral monilia is usually acquired from the mother as the infant passes through the vagina at birth. Thrush may disappear without treatment, but your doctor will probably want to give the baby medication for it three to four times a day. Treatment is especially important for breast-fed infants as the infection can spread to the mother's nipples and make nursing painful. Small red dots on the nipple are a symptom of yeast infection. If you think that you have the infection, obtain medication from your obstetrician to clear up the infection in the vagina as well as on the nipples.

While examining your baby's mouth, you may notice white blisters in the middle part of the lip. They are the result of vigorous sucking and will eventually go away by themselves.

Eyes

Years ago silver nitrate was dropped into a baby's eyes as a preventive measure against blindness from perinatal venereal disease. The silver nitrate frequently caused a mild inflammation and discharge in the eyes. Now penicillin has replaced silver nitrate for this purpose. A more frequent cause of infection in a baby's eyes is a plugged tear duct, which prevents tears from being drained off so they well up in the eye and run down the cheek. The eyelids may become mildly infected when the tears don't cleanse them properly. In most infants this condition clears up by the age of one, but your doctor will advise you if treatment is necessary.

However, a plugged tear duct does not cause the eye to look bloodshot or pinkish. If the white of the eye is discolored, you should call your doctor.

Umbilicus (Navel)

The umbilical cord contains two arteries and one vein. The cord is cut and tied after birth, but the opening doesn't completely close for almost a month. Infections of the umbilicus are especially serious because of the ease with which they can spread to the liver or abdominal cavity. Your doctor will probably ask that you clean the umbilical area with alcohol until the stump falls off. When this happens, you may safely give the baby a tub bath. It's important to follow your doctor's instructions carefully and notify him if you see any oozing, inflammation, or pus around the navel.

If you notice a swelling under the stump that protrudes when the baby cries, he may have an umbilical hernia. This occurs when the abdominal wall fails to close completely, and some of the abdominal contents protrude into the space formerly occupied by the umbilical cord. The size of the defect may range from less than a centimeter in diameter to as much as six centimeters. Many umbilical hernias are gone by the age of one, and most will have disappeared by the age of three. It used to be a common practice to bandage up the navel in an attempt to push it back into place, but now this practice has been largely abandoned in favor of surgery for those few cases in which the hernia hasn't closed by the age of five or six years. Even then surgery is only done if the hernia is troublesome and gets in the way of clothing.

Genitalia

It is not unusual for the breasts of a newborn male or female to be swollen and red. This is due to the actions of hormones present in the mother's blood before delivery. The swelling will subside without treatment, and it's wise not to massage or otherwise irritate the breasts.

These same maternal hormones may also produce a vaginal discharge in female infants. The discharge is usually creamy white but may be streaked with blood. The appearance can be startling, but there's really nothing to worry about, and the discharge stops in about a week.

In boy babies a swollen scrotum may be indicative of a hydrocele, a collection of fluid in the scrotum. Sometimes this condition will resolve spontaneously, or it may require surgical treatment. Your physician will advise you about this.

All these suggestions are meant to help you develop your own powers of observation. Each baby has special physical and personal characteristics that make him unique. By getting to know your baby and learning what his normal behavior is, you will be able to judge when something is amiss. Your pediatrician sees your child for only a few minutes during his checkup, and he depends on you to report anything unusual about the baby's behavior or appearance. Get to know your baby, and you will be doing the single most important thing in protecting his health and well-being.

How To Babyproof Your Home

by Dr. Harris D. Riley, Jr., and Karen Lohela Woodworth

Ten-month-old Michael can't walk yet. But he can climb up stairs, fall down stairs, stick pins in live outlets, chew anything he can get his hands on, choke, and reach for drugs and poisons.

The most important actions Michael's parents can take to protect him against accidental injury is to babyproof their home, which means preventing accidents by creating a home environment in which a baby can safely grow and be active.

Accidents are the leading causes of deaths in childhood, including the age period one to four years. Age is an important risk factor. For example, most accidental poisonings occur in children one to four years of age whereas injuries from firearms occur mainly in school-age children. During the first two years typical accidents include falls, inhalation of foreign objects, poisonings, burns, drownings, and motor vehicle accidents.

For young children the most dangerous place, ironically, is their own home. Serious accidents occur because parents, especially first-time ones, aren't always aware of the potentially dangerous situations in the home. Poisoning, for example, is one of the most common pediatric emergencies. New parents are usually aware of the need to store all household cleaning products, detergents, pesticides, and other recognized poisons out of their baby's reach. But other common and apparently harmless products such as baby and adult toiletries, deodorant, nail polish, and cosmetics can also poison a baby.

Growing up is a risky business for children. Everyday objects such as stairs and sharp utensils pose special dangers for babies and toddlers because they have no sense of danger yet, only great curiosity. Babies learn by exploring their environment, and without a knowlege of how to avoid accidents, they are headed straight for trouble.

That's why you should give your home a child safety checkup now. A good place to start is by reviewing the six safety lists below. There's one for each type of home accident involving children. Try working through one list each day for a week. By the end of the week, you will have succeeded in babyproofing your home and making it a safe place for baby to play.

Falls

■ Never leave an infant alone on a bed, changing table, or other high place. Severe falls are the most common form of injury to infants.

■ Barricade open stairways with safety gates. Creeping babies learn to go up stairs before they learn how to go *down* safely, so keep gates up until a child can manage well both ways.

■ Keep stairs free of objects that can cause you to trip while carrying the baby.

■ Look for wide-based, stable highchairs and walkers, use their seat belts, and don't let your child stand in a chair or climb into it himself.

■ Before a baby can pull himself up, lock the crib side rails at their highest level and adjust the mattress to the lowest position.

■ Keep low windows securely screened or locked.

■ When baby graduates to the big tub, skid-proof the bottom of the bathtub with nonslip stick-ons or a rubber mat.

■ When buying throw rugs, look for those with nonskid backing.

Fires And Burns

■ Keep hot liquids, hot foods, and cords of irons, toasters, and other appliances out of children's reach. Keep highchairs away from the stove and pot handles turned inward. Teach babies the meaning of "hot."

■ Reduce the setting on the hot water heater to 120°—hot enough to wash dishes yet not hot enough to scald a toddler who turns on the tap.

■ Buy a cold-water vaporizer, not a steamer. If yours does spout steam, place it where a sleepy child (or parent) won't run into it at night.

■ Buy flame-resistant children's clothes, especially sleepwear.

■ Store matches and lighters where curious toddlers can't get at them.

■ Screen fireplaces. Put guards around radiators and heaters.

■ Prevent electrical burns or shocks by unplugging unused extension cords. Sucking on the "live" end is a prime cause of electrical burns of the mouth. Put safety covers or heavy electrical tape over unused electrical outlets.

Poisoning

■ Keep all lethal household products on high shelves, not under the sink. Common household poisons include cleaning and polishing agents, waxes, detergents, lighter fluids, and all caustic or petroleum-based substances. In the basement or garage watch out for: paints, paint thinners, pesticides, weed killers, fertilizers, fuels and oils, car waxes, rust removers, mothballs.

■ Store cosmetic items like nail polish, hair spray, and deodorant out of children's reach.

■ Keep all prescription *and nonprescription* medicines in a high or locked cabinet. Buy bottles with childproof caps, and don't tell children that flavored medicines or vitamins are "candy."

■ Store alcoholic beverages out of children's reach. An overdose of alcohol in a child doesn't just cause a hangover—it can mean unconsciousness, brain damage, or even death.

■ Keep plants out of infant's reach. Eating (or sometimes just chewing) houseplants has surpassed ingestion of aspirin as a leading cause of accidental poisoning in young children. Common houseplants that are poisonous include caladium, coleus, dieffenbachia, hens and chicks, holly berries, jade, mistletoe berries, some philodendrons, poinsettia, and wandering Jew.

■ Use only lead-free paint or nontoxic finishes when repainting children's furniture, toys, or any other surfaces that might be chewed.

Choking

■ Toys for infants and toddlers should be too big to swallow and have no small, detachable parts. If stuffed animals or dolls have button eyes or ornaments that can be pulled off, remove them.

■ Don't let infants get at small objects that could be inhaled into the windpipe: coins, buttons and beads, marbles, snack foods like popcorn or nuts.

■ Always close safety pins, and set an example by never holding pins in your mouth.

■ Avoid propping bottles at feeding time. Babies can spit up, inhale the liquids, and choke.

Blows, Cuts, And Scrapes

■ Check baby furniture for any protruding screws or other sharp places.

■ Remove or push back from the edge of the shelf or table, any easily over-turned objects like lamps, plants, and heavy ornaments.

■ Substitute place mats for a tablecloth that hangs over the table edge so a toddler can't tug on the cloth and bring hot or heavy objects down on his head.

■ Never leave a cord from a lamp or appliance dangling where a baby could pull it and bring it down on himself.

■ Keep all sharp objects away from young children: knives, scissors, pins and needles, razor blades, tools.

Strangulation/Suffocation

■ Federal regulations now specify that crib and play yard slats should be no more than 2-3/8 inches apart, so that a baby can't slip feet first between the slats and get caught by his head. For cribs made before 1976 that don't meet these guidelines, add slats or use bumper guards tied on securely.

■ Place the crib away from drapery cords or electrical appliances.

■ Before baby can sit up, take down any cords holding toys strung across the crib. Toys hung on the sides of the play yard or crib should be on very short strings (6 inches or less) that can't wrap around baby's neck.

■ Never hang rattles or other objects around a baby's neck.

■ Don't give a young baby a pillow; he could suffocate.

■ Keep all plastic bags and plastic wrap away from young children. Never use thin plastic film on the crib mattress as a waterproof lining. A baby is helpless with thin, sticky plastic near his face; his inhaling creates a suction, which causes the filmy plastic to cling to his nose and mouth, cutting off air.

■ Use a firm mattress that fits snugly at the sides of the crib. If an adult can fit two fingers between the mattress and crib side, the mattress is too small and the baby's head could get wedged between the side rail and mattress.

■ Remove doors and lids from empty refrigerators and trunks.

Burn Prevention
by Jean Caldwell

Burns kill more children under the age of four than any in-fectious disease. Here's what you can do to protect your child from burn injuries.

That morning 16 years ago when she was burned is still etched in Barbara Enoch's memory.

"I was six years old. My friends and I were making scrambled eggs to surprise my mother. I was standing on a chair by the gas stove. The window was open. The breeze blew my short pajamas into the flame. I saw the flames leaping off the chair and started to take off the pajamas. That's how my hands were burned. But when I got the pajamas off and dropped them on the floor, they were just ashes.

"My friends were screaming. My mother ran in, and she began to scream. It was incredibly quick. At first I didn't realize I was hurt except for my back."

By the time neighbors had rushed her to the hospital, she remembers being very, very thirsty—a sign that vital fluids were pouring from the burned areas.

She suffered third degree burns on her hands, her neck, along her right arm, and down her right side to her waist. Her eyelashes and her hair were singed. One of the things that stands out in her mind is that her long hair had to be cut.

Barbara Enoch spent three months in the hospital. She still remembers the nightmares she had although time has dimmed the memory of pain. During her childhood and adolescence, she had to return for reconstructive surgery six times, and she has had two more operations recently to try to improve the ap-pearance of her scars.

She is a pretty, pixie-faced twenty-two-year-old Boston University graduate student and a student-intern at Shriners Burns Institute in Boston. She has come to grips with her scars, and she is fortunate that the flames did not burn her face. But she is disappointed that the last operation—undertaken purely for cosmetic purposes—did not turn out as well as she had hoped.

Major Health Problem

Burns are a public health problem of major proportions in this country. Some

12,000 people die in fires each year; 3,600 of them are children. In addition, over two million Americans suffer burn injuries.

Small children are particularly vulnerable. Burns kill more children under the age of four than cancer or any infectious disease. They are the leading cause of accidental deaths in the home, and outside the home; only automobile accidents claim more lives.

Contrary to popular belief, most children under two years of age who are burned suffer scalds or contact burns, not injuries from flames. In a study by the Shriners Burns Institute in Boston, flames injured three percent, chemicals another three percent, but a whopping 88 percent of the youngsters had been scalded or suffered contact burns.

How do little children sustain scalds or contact burns? Here are some cases taken from Shriners' files:

Jill was four months old. Her parents stopped by to visit friends. When they were asked to stay for dinner, they placed Jill on a blanket in a corner of the room where she could nap. After a while they heard her scream. She had rolled from her stomach to her back, and her arm was against the hot radiator. She suffered second degree burns to her right shoulder and upper arm. She was hospitalized for two days and returned daily to the clinic to have the dressing changed. She was left with a slight scar.

Steve was nine months old and learning to crawl. One night his teenaged uncle was baby-sitting for him. While the uncle was absorbed in his homework, Steve began sucking on the joint where a lamp was plugged into an extension cord. By the time his uncle noticed what was happening, Steve's mouth was severely burned. He suffered third degree electrical burns to the left side of his mouth and was hospitalized for six days. Over the next eight years, he was admitted to the hospital seven times for surgery to reshape his lip and to permit his mouth to open fully. He now has full use of his mouth, but his lip is still scarred and somewhat distorted.

Eleven-month-old Judy was just learning to walk. Her sister, Sally, was ironing and watching her. The phone rang. Sally turned off the iron and answered the phone. Judy watched, then suddenly lost her balance and in reaching out caught the cord of the iron. Baby and iron fell, and the hot, flat surface of the iron came to rest on Judy's bare shoulder. She was treated at the hospital as an outpatient for ten days for second degree burns to her shoulder.

Danny's family knew the wood stove in the family room was hot. His father had been hospitalized five days after burning his own palms when he tripped near a friend's stove the year before. To protect one-year-old Danny, the family erected a fence with a latching gate around the stove. One day Danny's mother left him in the hall while she stepped into an adjoining room. Thirty seconds later she heard Danny scream. He had gone into the family room. An older child had opened the gate to tend the stove and had forgotten to close it. Danny had both hands against the stove when his mother reached him. He was hospitalized for 13 days with third degree burns to the right palm and lesser burns to the left. He needed a skin graft for his right hand. Danny still wears a splint to keep his right hand from curling into a ball. Since his injury was recent, doctors do not know if he will need further surgery to retain full motion in his hand.

Fourteen-month-old Amy was delighted that it was bathtime. As her mother started to undress her, Amy's brother, who was sick in bed, called. Mother left Amy in the bathroom. Amy climbed onto the toilet and then up on the sink. She put her feet in the basin and turned on the water. It became boiling hot. Amy screamed. Her mother ran to the bathroom and pulled her out of the sink. Amy suffered second and third degree burns of both lower legs and feet. She was hospitalized for 37 days and needed surgery for skin grafts to her feet twice. Six months later her wounds were fully healed.

Two-and-a-half-year-old Paul was playing with his blocks on the kitchen floor. His mother asked Paul to put the blocks away because supper was almost ready. A few minutes later she picked up a pot of boiling spaghetti and started toward the kitchen sink to drain it. She didn't notice one block still lying in the middle of the floor. She tripped. The pot tipped and boiling water spilled over Paul. He was hospitalized two months with second and third degree burns over 65 percent of his body. He had two operations to graft skin over his burns. A year later he needed more surgery. He has permanent scars.

The Many Little Hazards

Hot liquids, hot grease, hot tap water, hot bath water, hot surfaces, and extension cord joints all burn small children. The studies made by Shriners Institute indicate that burns occur when the child explores without supervision—when the caretaker (mother, father, older sibling, baby-sitter) is rushed and distracted, under pressure—when the caretaker is not familiar with the child's ability to reach or climb or the speed with which the child can move, when the child grabs or leans against a hot object, reaches for a hot object, or bumps into someone carrying a hot liquid.

Sue Cahners and Muriel Sullivan, who are social workers at Shriners Burns Institute, were asked how parents could "learn not to burn" their children. Here are some of their observations about "the many little hazards many people are just not aware of."

Bath water is a frequent cause of serious burns and even death to small children. The problem is minimized if the cold water is run in first and then enough hot water added to make the bath comfortable. An adult hand is too insensitive to test bath water for an infant. The inside of the wrist is a better indicator. What might be a nice, hot bath for a tough, grown-up skin can burn a baby.

Infants as young as eight months can turn on a faucet. The rule "never leave a small child alone in the bathroom" serves to prevent both drownings and burns.

Small children find dangling electrical cords irresistible. They yank them and pull hot pots of coffee, irons, and toasters on top of themselves. Or they chew them and suffer electrical burns to the mouth.

A pot handle protruding over the edge of a stove can be yanked off by a small child. Remember: when it comes to safety, a child is not as tall as his head but as tall as his reach, say Cahners and Sullivan. It is also easy for an adult to bump into a protruding handle and spill the contents of a pot.

Bowls of soup, cups of tea or coffee may ruin a dress or trousers if they spill on an adult. If they spill on a small child, they can result in pain, hospitalization, and scars. Keep any container with hot food well back from the edge of the table.

If you must hold a small child in your lap at the table, drink something cold rather than something hot. A child who has been sitting perfectly still may suddenly reach out and knock over a cup of scalding coffee. Tablecloths are seldom thought of as a hazard. But small children like to pull on them, and in a second the coffee pot that was in the center of the table can be spilling over your toddler.

Barbecues are a common source of burns. White hot coals are deceptive. They are every bit as hot as flaming ones, but they don't look it. Many a child has tripped near a grill and fallen into the fire.

Household products such as drain cleaners can cause serious chemical burns. Cahners and Sullivan say these products are easy to open and are often stored under sinks where tiny children can find them.

The files of the Consumer Product Safety Commission in Washington record case after case where small youngsters touched, fell against, tried to climb on, tripped against, or were pushed against a hot wood stove. In every case the result was a burn serious enough for at least emergency room treatment.

Fire Prevention And Burn Treatment

The most common causes of house fires are a cigarette left smoldering on a sofa or chair, a carelessly discarded cigarette butt, a stereo that's been left on without music and then overheats, the instant-on TV, a frayed cord that causes a short circuit, and matches left where children can find them. Smoke detectors, of course, are a big help in alerting families to middle-of-the-night fires. These fires can result in suffocation or death when a panicky child hides under a bed or in a closet and is not found until it is too late.

Suppose you take every precaution and your child is still burned. What should you do?

First, extinguish the flames. Teach children to "drop and roll" if their clothes catch fire. Make them practice doing this because most people, including those who have been taught what to do, panic or run.

A blanket can smother flames, but don't waste time looking for one. Grab the child and roll him or her on the ground to extinguish the flames. Put cold water on the injured area. No water around? Cahners and Sullivan say that cold liquids, like those commonly available at a picnic, can help cool the injured area. Try milk, lemonade, carbonated drinks.

Remove burned clothing that isn't sticking to the skin. If the injury was a scald, remove all clothing. Remove rings and bracelets; swelling can follow a burn. Keep the burned person on his or her back. If the victim is having trouble breathing, place a pillow under the shoulder. Unless the burn is very, very slight, get medical attention at once. Burns are deceiving. They often look less serious than they really are.

It usually is not dangerous to move a badly burned person to a hospital. Children under fifteen can be admitted free to any of the three Shriners Burns Institutes—in Boston, Cincinnati, and Galveston, Texas. Ask your doctor if Shriners can help in any way if your child is burned. The Institutes offer both acute care immediately after an injury and reconstructive surgery in the years afterwards.

The Outlook For Burn Victims

Dr. John Crawford, chief pediatrician at Shriners in Boston, says that enormous advances in saving lives have been made in the last decades. Before 1943, when whole blood and plasma became available to treat shock, patients who were burned over more than 30 percent of their bodies died. By 1964, a few patients with third degree burns over 40 percent of their bodies were being saved. In the past two years, a few children survived with severe burns covering up to 90 percent of their bodies.

Advances such as the bacteria-free nursing unit have helped the badly burned patient. This is a plastic tent where bacteria-free air at 90 degrees Fahrenheit and with 90 percent humidity washes over the patient continually. This helps reduce the possibility of infection, which is one of the major complications with a burn.

New techniques also help patients cope with the loss of fluid from burned areas and have eliminated such post-burn complications as swelling of the brain, kidney failure, and Curling ulcer. In addition, Dr. Crawford reports that Shriners has made great strides in helping patients get enough nourishment. This may seem strange, but the nutritional requirements of a badly burned person are little short of astonishing. Someone trying to fight off infection and heal wounds over a large surface of his body may need as many calories as a lumberjack logging in the Maine woods in the middle of winter.

Skin banks provide a source of material to cover burns until grafts can be taken from the patient. Donor grafts are not permanent but do provide important temporary protection.

Dr. Crawford says, "We are doing better when it comes to reconstructing badly burned hands and faces." But one of the great misconceptions is that a plastic surgeon can make burned patients look the way they did before. Not so, says Crawford. The first aim of the surgeon is to restore function—to see that limbs move and that scar tissue does not contract joints.

In fact, the outlook for physical survival can be so good that according to Dr. Crawford, the quality of life for the burn survivor now becomes most important. A burned child can survive and be restored to full physical function only to die "a social death" because other children react badly to the scars. One of the most important aspects of treating a burned child is the attitude of adults outside the hospital, especially parents and teachers.

Social workers at Shriners exert every effort to help teachers understand the problems involved so they can help other children rise to the occasion and welcome back a burned classmate. Children who have been properly prepared beforehand often surprise skeptical parents by their acceptance of a badly burned friend.

But the staff at Shriners has a one-word answer if you ask for the very best treatment of burns: prevention.

Chapter 5
The Dilemmas of Parenthood

Guilt And The Working Mother
by Shirley L. Radl

There are mothers who work outside the home and feel no guilt whatsoever about that fact of their lives. I am aware of the existence of at least four of them. In contrast, I know dozens of working mothers who feel guilty and who worry about whether they are depriving their children. Backing up those I know personally are the many mothers I've never met but feel I know through the tortured letters they've written to me. Thus I've concluded that if guilt is generally built into the motherhood role, working mothers experience it even more intensely than mothers who stay home with their children.

Sadly, the women's movement notwithstanding, society does decree that a woman's place is in the home. It is a strong tradition that we live with—strong because it has been with us from the time we were little girls watching our mother's mothers, and strong because it is totally reinforced in all of the media. Even those of us who may truly believe that a woman's place is in the *world,* are subject, on a nearly reflexive basis, to the guilt and fear that grow out of the foundation of traditionalism.

Is Working Harmful To Your Children?

The working mother truly gets it from all sides, which is perhaps why she worries about what her working is doing to her children. And the fact that she is sensitive about working is perhaps why she is easy prey for disapproving friends, relatives, schoolteachers and nonworking mothers. And all of the criticism that she receives reinforces her fundamental fear that her working is going to prove to be damaging to her children, whom she does indeed genuinely love.

There is absolutely no evidence to support the notion that children are damaged or deprived when their mothers work. Dr. Mary Howell, a professor of pediatrics and associate dean of Harvard Medical School, studied 280 cases and concluded that the children of working mothers fared just as well as those of mothers who stayed home all day. Another study, conducted in 1970 by Dr. Mary Elizabeth Keister of the University of North Carolina, revealed that day-care children she studied from birth to five years were, if anything, slightly ahead of their peers

who were exclusively reared by their parents. She also found that in physical and emotional development, the children she studied showed no differences from their peers who were cared for exclusively by their parents.

In fact, numerous studies show that not only are children not damaged when their mothers work, but also they are likely to be well socialized if they go to pre-school groups and are apt to be independent and make good adjustments when they enter regular school. *Try as I might, I could not find one single study focused on average families that supported the old wives' tale that children are better off when mom stays home.*

At a more personal level, I do not know of a single child who has been damaged because his or her mother worked—and I know working mothers whose children cover virtually every age range.

When the disapproval and guilt are generously dished out, the working mother who absorbs it is laboring under the illusion that *all* mothers who stay home *always* do many things for their children. If you are a working mother, while you are castigating yourself, try to remember that your perceptions of what all homemakers actually do all day may be completely out of whack. Sure, some mothers are very involved with their children, but some are not. And some are so sick and tired of being with kids all the time that they just can't get up the energy to do as much with or for them as the average working mother does with hers. And remember, too, that some mothers who are trapped in the house are falling apart at the seams (which I suspect is far more hazardous to the mental well-being of their children than having sane working mothers might be).

Leading A Double Life

One does not have to be a perfectionist to experience a certain amount of schizophrenia at functioning in four separate and demanding roles. Not every working mother goes through this, but many do. And they say it is difficult to make the transition from office to home—that it is a dramatic one for them, and that there is really no time to shift gears. I do recall what it was like for me when I worked in an office. I remember coming home, often with work still on my mind, setting down my briefcase, hanging up my coat, and putting on an apron, all rather automatically while I halfway listened to the sitter tell me what had gone on and had a vague sense of lots of little hands pulling at my skirt. It was like culture shock. Often I wasn't completely clear in just what it was I was supposed to be doing. Oddly enough, until I talked to other working mothers about this, I thought I was unique, which of course led to the feeling that I was incompetent.

My advice to any working mother who is overwhelmed with guilt, child care, worry, and drudgery, is to take some time to catch her breath at the very first opportunity. Tell your employer that you need two days off to take care of some personal business—which is true enough. Then be sure you have child care (preferably outside the home) lined up. And then take one day and look at your routine and see what you can do to reduce the amount of time you must spend on it.

■ Make a list of household chores. Which of them can you pay someone else to do for you? Which, such as polishing silver, are not vital to maintaining reasonable cleanliness and order?

■ What errands do you run? Which of these could be accomplished with a phone call and a delivery service? The laundry and dry cleaners?

■ What things could you get your husband to do without arguing with him so long that it would cancel out any time you might save? Pay the household bills? Do the grocery shopping?

After you've made a reasonable assessment of how you can climb out of a horrendously demanding maintenance routine, then make as many arrangements as possible. *By phone!*

Buying services buys you time for yourself and time to spend with the family. It clears out enough of the fuzziness and confusion so that you can think constructively about what is really important—dealing with your feelings, your needs, and your children, and how all of that interrelates.

Spending Time With Your Children

When it comes to spending time with the children, some fathers who don't spend much of it may feel they are missing something, but it is doubtful that they feel *guilty* about it, as mothers often do. I think a whale of a lot of energy can be saved if a woman can accept that some things are more important to her than they may be to her husband. It is more useful to focus on the sorts of things that make her feel guilty about her children and employ some rather simple practices that can make both her and the children feel better. Here are just a few helpful suggestions—some of which apply equally for mothers who stay home —that can get you started thinking about what else might work for you:

■ First, remember that your working does not damage your children. Studies have proved that—tell yourself that every day and stop worrying about it. It makes you feel guilty to dwell on that, and guilt diminishes your effectiveness.

■ Making the transition from office to home is difficult. A mother can be physically present but actually absent because she's left her mind at the office. Children sense this and often, I think, respond to it with bratty behavior designed to get attention, which, of course, leads to more tension. Take a few minutes at the end of the workday to psyche yourself up for meeting with your children. Sometimes it helps to write down what is preoccupying you before you leave work and tell yourself that you'll forget it temporarily and look at it later in the evening when the children are in bed. Writing things down can get them out of your system temporarily.

■ If you can give your child (or each of your children) a few minutes of undivided attention at the end of your workday, quite likely you will find that five or ten minutes will be enough until there's a question or a need of some kind. The child will *take* the time in any case—a piece at a time possibly over a couple of hours. Usually children don't have that much to share with their parents, so if you give them what little they need for their forums, they feel that you care and are interested. And they go off and do something else, and you feel better. And, of course, father should do this too.

■ When your child wants to ask a question, tell you something, or show you something, and you are too busy, try this: tell him or her that you can't (whatever) at this time, but that in fifteen minutes, or when you finish writing this paragraph, reading this page, or chopping up this onion, you will. And then do it. This avoids his or her feeling rejected and your feeling guilty at having said, "I'm too busy," or "Don't bother me now."

■ If you feel you don't spend enough time with your child or children, block out some each week on your calendar—as you would a social engagement, an evening meeting, or some other appointment. My kids and I regularly make appointments with each other at the beginning of the week. They love it.

With younger children, you can spend a certain amount of time (say ten or fifteen minutes) several times a week, working a puzzle with big pieces that only takes so long—or playing a game or reading a short story. You don't have to spend whole hours at a time, and if you work this into your schedule or routine, you make the time for it and don't wind up in the position of having your child constantly begging you to play or read to him—which may result in your not doing so and feeling bad, or doing it and feeling resentful and bored.

Be Good To Yourself

All mothers, whether they work or not, need a day off now and then, apart from weekends and holidays that are spent with the family. It is usually guilt that holds them back from leaving children with a sitter for the sole purpose of having some time for themselves. This is especially so for the working mother, who may fear that she doesn't give her children enough of her time, and hence any days off should be spent with them. However, mothers must get into the habit of giving their own needs a high priority—by doing so, the time they spend with their children is more likely to be given freely and not with resentment. So, if you can't be good to yourself *for* yourself, do it for your kids.

To Spank Or Not To Spank

by Shirley L. Radl

"As regards spanking in particular—even though it may be a great tension reliever—I see it as appropriate only when it is part of a parent's overall approach to discipline. And that overall approach should include the healthy expression of feelings and the making and enforcement of reasonable rules."

In sifting through most of the child-guidance literature aimed at parents, it becomes clear that spanking is seen by most experts as an integral part of parenting. Fitzhugh Dodson, for example, has much to say on the subject. In *How To Parent,* he starts by pointing out that you don't calmly tell a child who runs in front of a car not to do it again; instead you reinforce the command with a few healthy smacks. And he continues: "I believe it is impossible to raise children effectively—particularly aggressive, forceful boys—without spanking them." Dr. Dodson claims that he has never met a parent who does not get angry, and that even though most parents can smoothly handle even their difficult offspring, he acknowledges that "there are times when the slightest annoying thing a child does is enough to set us roaring at him."

Maintaining that it is important for parents to give honest expression to their feelings, Dr. Dodson then says: "The main purpose of spanking, although most parents don't like to admit it, is to relieve the parent's frustration. All of us need to do this from time to time when our kids get on our nerves....We get fed up when our kids misbehave, and we lose our cool and swat them. But that's nothing to feel guilty about. We feel better and they feel better. The air is cleared."

Even Benjamin Spock, often criticized for his permissive attitude, maintains that "the air is cleared" when a parent gives vent to anger by spanking a misbehaving child. And he believes that the only time a parent should spank is when he or she is angry: "You sometimes hear it recommended that you never spank a child in anger but wait until you have cooled off. That seems unnatural. It takes a pretty grim parent to whip a child when the anger is gone."

And yet—even with the sanctions from these two very well-known experts (and many others)—there are many parents who don't spank even when the child seems to be begging for it. Some parents don't spank simply because they don't discipline their children at all. Other parents don't spank because they are uncomfortable about hitting another person. And then there are some parents who don't spank their children because, at least for themselves, they subscribe to the view of those who say you should "never spank a child in anger."

When Spanking Goes Too Far

In explaining why this is her rule, one mother told me, "When I'm really mad — and I mean mad—at my daughter, nothing could make me hit her—one slap and I'd be done for because it wouldn't end there."

"There is a fine line between discipline and child abuse," said another mother. "There are times when I know if I start hitting, I'll just keep hitting, so at our house, we don't hit in anger."

I have run from my kitchen in the heat of the battles that occur when the pots are simmering on the stove and the energetic juices of my children have brought *me* to the boiling point. I can't tell you why, but I have known that if, at such a time, I were to give in to a nearly irresistible impulse to hit, it wouldn't stop with a mere spanking.

The one thing shared by angry parents who feel like hitting but don't, is the absolute knowledge that a spanking, initiated at the wrong moment, might turn into a beating. Some parents know this because it has happened to them; some just know it instinctively. One who speaks from sad experience puts it this way: "It starts out, I think, as honest discipline, and before you know it, you start feeling better as you hit and you keep going—and at some point it becomes nearly impossible to stop. After that happened to me, I began seeing the urge to spank as a warning—so I don't spank."

The experiences of these parents, I think, can be compared to the experiences that occur in certain therapy groups when patients are encouraged to work through feelings of hostility by hitting a pillow with fists or "encounterbats." The pillow is supposed to represent someone for whom the patient feels present or past anger. I watched one woman take on the pillow. She started out by giving it a half-hearted swing, then slowly, she began repeating the name of the person at whom her anger was directed. Soon she was screaming, crying, and punching with all her might. The more she called the pillow "Ralph," and angrily told "him" why she was so angry, the angrier she became, hitting harder and harder and with more frequency. Having allowed herself to let go of her feelings, she appeared unable to control them—the first few hits had released furies she wasn't conscious of.

When, after about 10 or 15 minutes, her rage had subsided, the pillow was completely flattened out. It was only a pillow, of course, but I have no reason to doubt that to this woman, it was indeed Ralph. Or that had it been Ralph, she would have behaved any differently once she really felt her rage.

Social Pressures

This woman, like parents who fear they will lose control, had a storehouse of unresolved anger that she had not expressed at the appropriate times. And parents who carry around these "storehouses" carry around not only unexpressed anger, but quite possibly, unacknowledged anger as well. And they reach a point where all of it can be triggered by a simple, annoying act on the part of the child. Thus, for example, when a mother becomes enraged because her four-year-old tips over a glass of milk, she may later explain her disproportionate rage by saying that it was "the final straw." But what made it "the final straw" was that she did not acknowledge or express her feelings when the irritating incidents occurred. And she may explain *this* by saying that she was trying to be patient and understanding and not pounce on her child every time he did something that bothered her. And she may actually believe this. But I don't.

I think, instead, there is another reason why many parents neither recognize nor express their feelings at the moment they feel them. Patience is not the inhibiting factor. Nor is the fact that nearly every child-guidance specialist acknowledges parental wrath. I think that it is because the *prevailing* social attitude is that *normal* parents are *never* supposed to feel anger toward their children.

When, for example, was the last time you saw a really angry parent on television? Even an *unhappy* one? When was the last time you saw a child throw a tantrum or a bowl of cereal across the room in a commercial, situation comedy, or soap opera? When was the last time you saw parental anger outside of a documentary on domestic violence?

It is an open question whether the mass media shapes current attitudes or reflects them. Either way, our media certainly reinforces the notion that children are always well-behaved and parental wrath is nonexistent.

In fairness, I don't really think that it is the intent of the mass media or advertisers to convince people that family life is perfect and devoid of anger. But they do. And the image they project cannot fail to be received by most of us.

Anger And Guilt—A Vicious Cycle

When parents repress their anger because it's not socially acceptable, they become further angered by their very repression, and a new cycle of anger is set in motion. The average parent today labors under the illusion that he or she should never feel anger, should never spank a child, and should be able to control a child, yet never need to. And when fully convinced she should never feel anger, a mother may feel the accumulation of unacknowledged and unexpressed emotion to such an extent that she finds herself on the brink of violence. And being there may well add another dimension to her wrath—she may become even angrier over having been made to feel that way in the first place. And at this point, no matter *what* she does about it—whether she hits or walks away—she's bound to add to her storehouse a certain amount of guilt. The cycle is now complete.

So what's an angry mother to do?

I think that first, any mother who senses that spanking might trigger a storehouse of anger would do well to trust her instincts. While it may be important to express anger, I think that clearly this is one occasion when it is far wiser to walk away—and pat yourself on the back for doing so. None of us really want to do harm, and none of us want to live with the remorse over having punished a child too severely for a trivial transgression.

After walking away, a reasonable course of action is to resolve to pay attention to angry feelings as they occur and resist the temptation to put a value on them. Don't, for example, tell yourself how petty you are to be angry at an innocent child. And don't tell yourself you shouldn't feel that way—it is pointless, because, as any psychiatrist will tell you, you feel as you feel, and no command or injunction can change that.

Give voice to anger when it is felt. Talk to a friend and let off steam. Call a hotline. Tell your child that you're "so mad you can't see straight." Stamp your foot and yell.

The Fear Of Emotional Abuse

But, you might be thinking, *really* yelling at my child means I'll be guilty of emotional abuse. Yet that's another reason for the tension and frustration you're feeling. Besides everything else, lurking somewhere in the background is the fear that if you express your anger when you feel it, you will emotionally abuse your child.

To begin with, I think that many conscientious and intelligent parents have gotten the idea that virtually anything they do will somewhat result in some sort of abuse. And that, for example, a parent who has screamed at a child, "You are bad," "You are stupid," "You drive me crazy" and done so *even but once,* fully believes that he or she has committed a grievous sin and programmed a child for life. Given the way in which the term "emotional abuse" is bandied about, there isn't a parent alive who hasn't been guilty of it—or, for that matter, experienced it personally during his or her own childhood.

But emotional abuse is far more complicated than occasionally flying off the handle and hurling insults we will later regret. Emotional abuse is not the same as an occasional outburst of anger. Instead, it consists of habitually demeaning and insulting a child, neglecting him, withholding affection, and threatening him with abandonment. It also can involve the sort of physical abuse that leads to serious injury. Emotional abuse, briefly, is a combination of cruelty and indifference—not seeing to a child's basic needs for physical and emotional well-being.

In my own experience, for example, I cannot help but wonder how it is possible that telling my son he's really bad news—only once—could program him for life, when having told him a thousand times not to take my scissors has had virtually no impact. (Especially since I do not in any way mean it when saying the former but absolutely and emphatically mean it when saying the latter.) All of this has led me, as a parent, to believe that it is important to develop perspective in order that the fear of abuse doesn't lead to it.

Some Solutions

I have no definitive answers for every parent, but I can share some of my own perspective. As regards spanking in particular—even though it may be a great tension reliever—I see it as appropriate only when it is part of a parent's overall approach to discipline. And that overall approach should include the healthy expression of feelings and the making and enforcement of reasonable rules. Spanking, to me, is a last resort to drive home an important point and not an end result of unrepressed rage. It isn't the fault of my children, for example, that the culture has told me that anger is an unacceptable emotion, or that even those experts who recognize its existence have never offered suggestions for holding it. But I do see that spanking may be appropriate on occasion—a well-placed and safe parental whack as an attention-getting device when your voice just doesn't make it.

And there are times when I think that spanking is clearly unwise and potentially dangerous. At the top of the list is that occasion when a parent senses that anything physical might lead to violence. Following very closely behind are those instances when a child's behavior is beyond his control. Such things as toilet training problems, bed-wetting, or regression (in older children) of bowel habits, for example, can drive parents right up the wall. But most of the time, these are problems that no amount of discipline or punishment can change. In the instance of the last two, these are often physical problems, and the way to deal with them is to consult a doctor and let him prescribe.

I think these rules generally apply to accidents. After having just gone through a period where, because I had read just enough psychology to turn a little bit of knowledge into a dangerous thing, I found myself looking for underlying motives in virtually everything my children did. Now, however, I accept spilled milk or a broken dish at face value—such clumsy acts are no longer seen as having been designed to goad me.

To do no harm is a goal that begins with the acceptance of anger as a normal human emotion. As one learns to acknowledge anger and not see it as something to be ashamed of, the tendency to store it away in what Theodore Rubin (*The Angry Book*) calls a "slush fund" will diminish. One should develop a pattern of dealing with old anger and recognizing and expressing feelings as they come up. Ultimately, according to Dr. Rubin, acknowledgment alone can become a form of expression, with nothing more being required to give release to the emotion. It is, Rubin reminds us, when we deny negative feelings that they turn into festering poisons.

And when a parent reaches that point where the anger that is felt relates only to what is taking place at the moment, then a spanking will consist only of a well-placed swat, meted out to emphasize the verbal discipline that is appropriate.

Meanwhile, to get rid of anger, try hitting something else. How about a pillow named Ralph?

The Crucial Years For Father And Child
by Doug Spangler

Many recent articles and books tell us that the first few years of a child's life are crucial for her intellectual development. The authors would have us believe that a child's early intellectual stimulation is the most important thing to be concerned about as parents.

Actually there's something even more *basic and* more *significant for your child's total personal development. What is it? A great deal of research in the field of child development shows that a truly loving parent-child relationship is a necessary foundation for all your child's present and future growth, including intellectual growth. Thus it's your relationship with him that you should really concentrate on.*

Dr. T. Berry Brazelton, well-known pediatrician and author, recently put the priorities in order: "Real affective, or emotional, interaction between parent and child is more important than the cognitive 'kick' that everybody's into right now. I think that's important too, but I think *it comes second to the other*" (italics mine.)

No doubt you intend to develop a personal relationship with your child anyway. The question is, when is the crucial time to begin?

If you're like me, you didn't start out asking yourself this question. Before my first child was born, I thought I'd become closely involved with him when he got to be around three or four years old. I assumed that the mother is most important to the child at first and that the father makes his contribution later.

Perhaps you've thought this too. But is this assumption correct?

Absolutely not! In fact, research evidence is overwhelming that you, the father, are vitally important to your child *from her very first day of life.* According to Michael and Jamie Lamb (in their article "The Nature and Importance of the Father-Infant Relationship," *The Family Coordinator,* October 1976): "Fathers are important in the eyes of their infants, and...they have an important role to

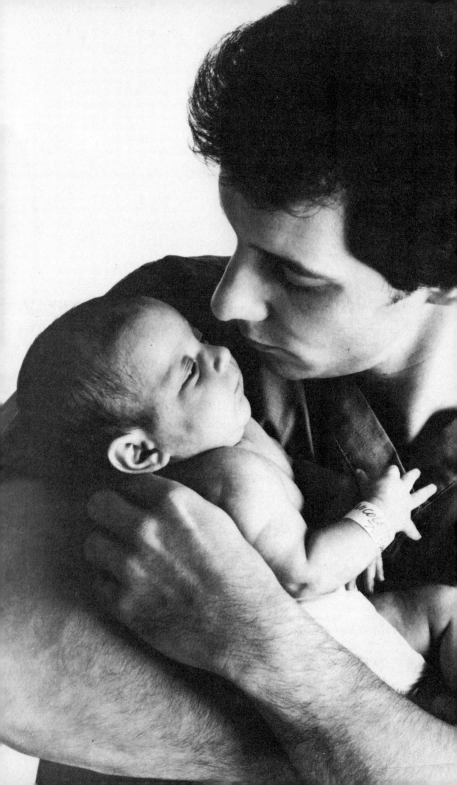

play in the socialization of their children from infancy onwards...The relationships infants experience with their fathers and mothers differ in quality, involve different sorts of interaction, and consequently...fathers, like mothers, have the potential for a significant...impact on the psychological and social development of their infants.''

Furthermore, Dr. Lee Salk reports in *What Every Child Would Like His Parents To Know,* ''Research conducted on children whose fathers were away in military service revealed that...boys whose fathers were *absent during the first year of life* seemed to have had *more behavior difficulties* than would normally have been expected. They seem to have had more trouble establishing and keeping good relationships, not only with adults but with other children. Other studies showed a reasonably close relationship between delinquent behavior in boys and the absence of an adequate father (male) figure during childhood'' (italics mine).

You might think these findings are extreme. They aren't. Additional studies indicate that the results are the same whether the father is absent or whether he's present but generally weak and ineffectual. In fact, as Dr. Salk points out, ''Having a father around who is weak and who does not take responsibilities with his child can sometimes be worse than having no father at all.''

Obviously then, your relationship with your child is crucial from the beginning. Your infant needs *you*, especially during his first few years. But how do you actually go about developing your relationship with your youngster? Here are three helpful ways:

Be In Contact

I'll never forget the first time I handled a baby. My niece looked so small, so fragile. I was sure she must be too tender for my rough, inexperienced hands. I felt the same way years later when my firstborn arrived. I was so anxious about making a mistake. It seemed easier just to avoid the whole issue and let my wife handle the baby by herself.

Fortunately, I didn't fall into this trap. And I quickly found that not only did I like holding my baby, but also he enjoyed being in contact with me. As time went on I discovered many ways to be in contact with my kids: hugging, cuddling, comforting and kissing them, massaging them or scratching their backs, feeding them, dressing them, changing their diapers, bathing them, holding and reading to them, wrestling and dancing with them, talking to them and carrying them places. My physical touch was the first way—and will always be a major way—to express my affection for my kids.

But there is more than just physical contact involved in your relationship with your child. We fathers must also strive for *emotional* contact. This means getting beneath the physical, active part of your child to the emotional, feeling side—to his personality, his self. It means, for example, communicating to your child that you love him and accept him as a fellow human being in his own right (not as a smaller version of you). It means helping her to know that you are affected by her and by what she does and thinks. It means showing him that you care enough to nurture him through all the changing experiences of his life.

Increasing your emotional involvement in the nurturing relationship becomes even more important to your child as she grows up. Research bears this out. For example, Biller and Meredith, in *Father Power*, report, ''Psychologists have discovered that fathers of low-achieving children are likely to be just the opposite of those of achieving children. Such fathers are frequently rejecting, critical, don't think much of themselves, and *aren't really emotionally involved in their children's lives''* (italics mine).

Be Together

Of course, if you plan to be truly nurturing to your child, you must spend significant amounts of time with her. Often when we fathers translate this goal into reality, it turns out that we take our kids someplace on the weekend and call that ''togetherness.'' But chances are these trips include more than you and your child (perhaps your other children and your wife go along). And your focus is usually on some event (a baseball game, errands, shopping, the zoo, or a playground) instead of on your child.

I used to think I was performing my fatherly duty doing things ''together'' with the kids that way. But then I read in Dr. Lee Salk's *What Every Child Would Like His Parents to Know*, '':...A child gets a certain sense of satisfaction out of being alone with his father. All too often a well-meaning father gathers all of his children together and plans a group excursion. While this can be enjoyable and rewarding, I think you should recognize that each child needs to get to know each of his parents alone.''

When I tried this approach, I soon saw the wisdom of what Dr. Salk was saying. It *is* a much different experience when you share special times with each child, by *himself*. You get to see your child in a completely different light, without the distractions and pressures of his siblings. And you can recognize and appreciate his uniqueness all the more.

So now I try to spend a little time alone with each of my kids every day. Sometimes we talk, maybe read a book, cuddle or wrestle, or perhaps we play with toys. My aim is just to enjoy being together. I have to admit that because of my work and family schedules, we don't always get our special together-time each day; but I keep it as a goal and manage to achieve it most of the time.

Be 100% Present With Your Child When You're With Him

In addition to *how much* time you spend together, it's important to consider *what* you do when you are with your child. I know from personal experience that it's very easy to be with your child bodily but to be far away in your thoughts. Many times problems on the job, mental lists of chores to accomplish, worries about money, work to be done on the car, or the desire to pursue my own hobby, will draw my thoughts from the child I'm with. I also know from personal experience that you can't hide this inattention from your child. He'll holler "Daddy!" and bring you back to him, or he'll fade out of the activity.

Developing your relationship with your child means you must strive to be 100% present with her. It means you have to suspend *your* problems and concerns for the time being and avoid distractions (turn off the TV, put down the news-papers, and so on). It means focusing your full attention on what she is saying or doing and responding appropriately. It means attempting to understand her behavior, her thoughts, her likes and dislikes. It means being free and relaxed enough to get to know *her*.

When you aren't 100% present with your child, your relationship becomes superficial. You lose touch. I saw this demonstrated at my daughter's preschool. The parents of one girl asked the preschool teachers what the child would like to have for her birthday. Evidently they had not spent enough "100 percent time" with the girl to even know what her play preferences were or to understand her developmental level.

I've also found that the more I know about child development all the way along the line, the more I'm able to understand each of my children individually. It enables me to put their behavior in perspective, to listen with the "third ear" to feelings behind their words, and to help them grow through the various stages.

But listening to and understanding your child is only half of being 100% present. It's only half of developing a positive relationship. You must talk *with* him, not just *to* him, honestly sharing your thoughts, feelings, and interests. Believe me, your child wants and needs to know you-the-person, not just you-the-parent.

For us fathers, it all boils down to priorities. Sure, there are many important concerns that tug at us daily and demand our attention and energies. But a close, positive interaction with each child now during her first few years of life is crucial for her entire personal development. Knowing this, then, let's resolve to make ourselves and our time available, and make every day a Father's Day.

Parent Support Groups:
A Place To Turn For Help
by Diane Mason

When new parents feel frustrated or alone, self-help organizations offer comfort and information.

It is midnight, and an anxious young mother is dialing the telephone. Standing nearby is her husband, holding their wailing infant. After a friendly voice answers, the mother begins.

"My son has been crying for two hours, and we just don't know what to do. We've tried feeding him, rocking him, changing him—nothing works!"

"You must be exhausted! How old is he?"

"Two weeks."

"Does he seem sick or feverish?"

"No," answers the mother.

"It's always frustrating when a baby cries and we can't figure out why," the volunteer begins. Then she suggests techniques for holding the baby and massaging him to relieve possible gas pains from colic or swallowed air. She sympathizes with the parents' plight and assures the mother that her feelings are normal. When the mother starts to sound calmer, the volunteer asks the parents to phone her in 30 minutes if the techniques described don't work.

Telephone-support systems like this one are part of a new network of parents' groups that are reaching out to help new parents. Often called "hot lines" or "help lines," these systems are staffed by parent volunteers who are trained to answer nonmedical questions about infant care. When a new mother or father feels frustrated, alone, or at a loss, the parents' group provides a place to turn and a source of information and comfort. In Santa Barbara, California, an organization called PEP (Postpartum Education for Parents) offers its "warm line" on a 24-hour basis. Such services can become an emotional lifeline to parents who are reluctant to bother their pediatricians on off hours or who just need some plain, old-fashioned encouragement.

Among the new parents services offered by "Great Expectations" of Portage,

Indiana, are monthly get-togethers for mothers interested in talking and sorting out their ideas and mixed feelings about parenthood. Baby-sitting is provided free. At a program called "Kidstuff," sponsored by CAPE (Childbirth and Parent Education of Kansas City, Missouri), mothers bring their preschoolers together for songs and crafts. Then the kids continue their projects with one of the members while the rest of the moms split off for discussion. The PACE Association of New Orleans, Louisiana, calls its monthly meetings "Mothers' Circle," and in Tulsa, Oklahoma, a group named Childbirth and Family Life offers parents' programs entitled *After Baby Comes* (ABC).

The Childbirth and Parent Education Association (CPEA) of Madison, Wisconsin, which has been offering services to parents for many years, created an organizational arm called "Bereaved Parents." Here, parents who have lost a child find hope and compassion from other parents who have gone through the same tragedy. Like other similar groups, they offer self-help discussions, telephone support, and referrals to professionals.

The success of groups that helped educate women about Cesarean delivery led to the establishment of a national organization for this purpose. C/SEC (Cesarean/Support, Education and Concern) provides information and resources to local groups who want to develop this type of service.

Parent Education

Parents' groups have also become centers for parent education. Film showings, speakers, and workshops are popular. Many programs resemble a school for parents, such as the six-week class sponsored by the Maternity-Family League of Indianapolis, Indiana, open to couples with babies under one year of age.

What is happening in these groups, and in others like them throughout the country, suggests a dramatic change in the way parenting will be viewed in the years to come. And more important than the way we perceive parenting is the action we take toward improving the skills it requires.

What makes today's parents different from their predecessors? Why do new parents feel a greater need to form organizations and alliances, and why are child development experts telling us that parent self-help groups will play a major role in the future of family life?

That we live in a changing society is obvious. Families are more mobile; new parents often find themselves isolated from their own parents and family members. Neighbors come and go, and close, long-time friendships are harder to establish. Yet while these are major causes of the stress that modern families face, another, perhaps more significant, change is taking place.

Parents are looking at themselves and their roles in a new way. Attitudes toward child rearing are shifting from a belief that parenting is instinctive to a realization that parenting is a learned skill, and one for which there is little preparation.

We have been making the mistaken assumption that when a baby is born, a signal sounds that magically, immediately transforms us into experienced, confident mothers and fathers. Now parents are willing to admit that their signals simply didn't go off and that they need help.

Burton White, Ph.D., author of *The First Three Years of Life* and founder of the Harvard Preschool Project, writes:

''...today, people who are about to have their first child feel no shame in saying out loud, 'I would like to have some information about this job, and I would like to know where I can get the help I will need in order to do it well.' People were not comfortable saying anything like that until five or ten years ago.''

Now parents are forming organizations to meet these needs. By banding together in caring, supportive alliances, both new and seasoned parents are discovering a common ground and a way to help each other improve their parenting skills. Parents' groups have, in a sense, become a substitute for the extended family.

What The Groups Can Offer

First, these groups provide a community of peers—other parents who are facing the same problems and searching for solutions. Parents learn from each other by exchanging ideas about child rearing. And while each group has a focus that meets its members' needs, there seems to be one common motive in all such organizations: a commitment to positive solutions and to bolstering the self-esteem of those who have chosen the role of parent. Parenting is important enough to learn about in an organized way, and by so doing, we are improving family life for ourselves and for our children.

Second, a parents' group can offer educational opportunities. Through various methods such as workshops and group encounters, it becomes a forum for examining a variety of alternatives to child rearing. Depending upon the resources of the group, members may even have the opportunity to learn new ideas from experts and professionals in fields relating to child development and family life.

Parents' groups always provide a place to turn. What a new or troubled parent most often needs is a compatriot—someone to say: "I understand how you feel. I've felt that way too," or "That happened to me." Some of our greatest stress is relieved when we become aware that we are not alone and that our frustrations and anxieties are normal. Often another parent is the only person who can give us the assurance we need. To support and be supported is what parents' groups are all about.

All generations have believed that the family is important. But what is happening today is an affirmation of that belief and a declaration of the interdependence of families and society. Today's parents, in particular, need new tools to cope with a traditional, yet changing, role. Parents' groups will furnish such a tool.

Who can start a parents' group? Anyone. It can be large or small; it can function solely to meet its members' needs, or it can extend its reach to the whole community. It doesn't require grants or special funding to survive—it can thrive on its own members' efforts. Its legacies will be parents who have a place to turn, who have the opportunity to investigate a variety of approaches to parenting, who can learn new techniques and ideas about child rearing, and who have gained confidence through a union of peers.

And the ultimate beneficiaries will, of course, be our children.

Telling Children About Death
by Phyllis Evans

What they should know and how to tell them.

When five-year-old Tommy's grandmother died, his parents told him that "Grandma went away for a while." During the funeral and family gatherings, Tommy was sent to a neighbor's house. A few weeks later, Tommy began asking his parents when his grandmother would return and why his grandfather "didn't go away with Grandma too."

Tommy's parents didn't want to burden him with the unpleasantness of death. They felt he was "too young to be exposed to such things." However, most child psychologists feel that there is no time like the present to discuss death with children.

Since one out of 20 children loses a parent before he finishes elementary school and inevitably faces the death of a close friend or relative during childhood, most experts advise parents to expose their children to the concept of death before it hits home.

According to Suzanne Ramos, author of *Teaching Your Child to Cope With Crisis,* sheltering a child from death will ultimately hurt him later in life. Ms. Ramos says that if a child does not understand that death is part of the life cycle, he will be unable to cope with death later on in life.

At what age should the concept of death be introduced to children? According to child psychologist Dr. Lee Salk, a child is unable to understand the notion of death before the age of two and a half. Even then, he might only use words such as kill or dead without really understanding their meaning. By the age of three or four, a child is ready to begin to grasp the meaning of death, although a real understanding probably will not occur until a specific death is discussed.

How should the concept of death be introduced to children? A group of psychiatrists at the Princeton Center for Infancy and authors of *The Parenting Advisor* suggest that the death of a distant friend or relative be mentioned to children so that they gradually become accustomed to the subject. When a parent sees a dead bird or animal in the street, he should stop to explain to the child what has happened. The PCI strongly recommends pets for young children for this reason, as well as for many others. If a pet that a child loves dies, he can be taught to mourn the pet. As a result, the child will be taught that sadness follows death. Finding a special box for the animal and performing a private funeral and burial will teach children the rituals following death. But the PCI warns parents not to replace the dead pet too quickly—a child must learn that the loved one cannot be easily replaced.

After observing and hearing about the death of a distant person, a child will be ready to cope with a death closer to home. If a family member is seriously ill, parents should be sure to explain this to a child. Don't hide any of the facts, because children are unusually perceptive and sense that something is wrong when they overhear hushed whispers and observe looks of concern.

It is essential to teach a child the meaning of mourning. Encourage him to express his feelings of sadness. Let him see you cry, and tell him that it is okay and acceptable to feel sad. Remember to talk about the dead person, telling a child that even though their grandmother, uncle, or pet will not be coming back, they still have many happy memories to talk about. It is important that parents allow a child to take part in giving away the clothes or mementos of the deceased. Giving a child a special memento of the dead person, such as a piece of jewelry, may alleviate his sadness and keep memories of the beloved alive.

Should a child attend the funeral? Ms. Ramos says that children between the ages of four and eight should attend the funeral, if only for five minutes. Children over eight should attend all services, and children under four should be encouraged to express their feelings of grief, but probably will not understand what is taking place at a funeral, according to Ms. Ramos.

She does, however, suggest that a parent use his own discretion if hysterics or anything that may be overly frightening to a child, is expected.

A parent's own feelings must determine whether a child should view the body of a dead person. In *About Dying* by Sara Bonnett Stein (in cooperation with The Center for Preventive Psychiatry in White Plains, New York), Ms. Stein writes that a child may find it easier to say good-bye to a body rather than a coffin. However, seeing the body of a dead person can also traumatize a child, and many experts caution parents to avoid having their children view an open coffin or be present when the coffin is lowered into the ground. This is a decision each parent must carefully make, taking into account his own child's ability to handle the situation.

Each child reacts differently to death, and feelings of anger and guilt are not uncommon. A child may lash out in anger against the dead person asking, "Why did Aunt Martha have to die?" or exclaiming, "I hate them!" A parent should explain that the person was very sick, or old, or that they had an unfortunate accident, but that there was a reason they died.

Children sometimes don't understand the difference between reality and fantasy and may believe that they caused the person to die because they "wished" them dead by once saying, "I hate you," or "I wish you were dead!" Parents must explain to a child that she had nothing to do with causing the death; otherwise a child may suffer feelings of guilt and torment.

A child may also fear abandonment. He will wonder if his mother or father will die and leave him alone. If your child asks, "Mommy, are you going to die?" tell him that eventually everyone does, but reassure him that "I take good care of myself so that I will live a long, long time."

Often children find it difficult to express their feelings of unhappiness, and they react callously to death. They will make a point of laughing and being naughty to cover up their real feelings. Sit down with your child, and tell him it is normal to be distressed when someone dies.

Never hide the truth from a child or try to protect him from death. As in the case of five-year-old Tommy, who began asking a lot of questions about his grandmother, children are inquisitive and are not easily satisfied by vague answers. Children find it hard to understand that death is final and forever, and that the dead person is not coming back. Instead of telling a child that "Grandma is going away for a while," tell him that "I know you will miss Grandma, but she won't be coming back."

Never tell a youngster that a dead person "has gone to sleep" or is "resting permanently." As a result, a child might fear going to sleep or being in a dark room.

Children may ask many questions about the dead person. "Where is he now?" "Does it hurt to be dead?" or "Why is he in the ground?" are just some of the questions that might come up. If a parent is too upset to discuss these things with a child or is overcome by grief, experts suggest counseling for the child.

Each person's religious beliefs will influence the way in which he tells his child about death, since every religion has its own interpretation of life and death. If you have already introduced your children to the concept of religion and your particular beliefs, you may want to let those beliefs enter into a discussion about death. A child who is not familiar with such ideas will not be comforted by religious explanations of death, especially if they are suddenly mentioned for the first time.

When Betty was seven years old, her grandmother died. Her parents felt it was best not to tell her "because she should be spared the unhappiness." Today Betty is a grown woman who still resents the fact that she wasn't honestly told about her grandmother's death or allowed to attend the funeral with the rest of her family.

"I always resented not taking part in my grandmother's funeral, and when I was much older and my father died, I had a difficult time coping with the harsh reality of death," Betty admits.

In her *Open Family Book Series*, Sara Bonnet Stein compares childhood immunizations, which hurt a little but prepare the child to face bigger threats in life, to exposing a child to bigger crises, such as death. Most experts today agree that instead of protecting or sheltering a child from crisis, he should be told the truth. Words of encouragement and understanding will help children learn about death and will equip them with the strength and courage that they will eventually need in order to face the realities of life and death on their own.

Sex And The New Parent
by Jean Gochros

"We thought that having a baby would give new meaning and joy to our lovemaking. But suddenly everything's all wrong! What's the matter with us?"

This is a frequent complaint of new parents but one that is seldom dealt with adequately; with all the advice given, it seems surprising that so little is given about sex. Many couples, told only that intercourse can be resumed after a specified time following delivery, are dismayed to find unexpected problems cropping up. Inadequately informed and embarrassed to ask questions or to discuss the problem, they too often assume that something terrible is wrong, and their worry compounds the problems. Here are some of the questions and concerns that couples seem to have, with some answers and suggestions for achieving a happier sexual relationship.

Q. "We were told not to have intercourse for four weeks, but I'm eager for it now. Is it OK? Am I abnormal or oversexed?"

A. It's ironic that one of the most common problems is really "no problem." While many doctors suggest refraining from intercourse for four or more weeks following delivery, this is an arbitrary date based on an "average" length of time it takes to recover or often chosen mainly to coincide with the follow-up visit. Although you should certainly check with your doctor before going ahead, intercourse can often be resumed within two to three weeks or whenever the amount of bleeding and discomfort decreases enough for the woman to find coitus enjoyable.

Don't hesitate to ask your doctor. Many people deny themselves or worry unnecessarily because they are afraid to ask a legitimate question. Of even more concern is the fact that many women, guilt-ridden because they've "disobeyed," don't make their follow-up visit, causing themselves needless nonsexual medical problems.

Q. "Since I'm nursing, I can't get pregnant, right?"

A. Wrong! Before resuming intercourse, discuss contraception with your doctor. If using the rhythm method, make doubly sure you understand instructions, for that method is especially unreliable during the first few months after childbirth.

Q. "When the baby nurses, I get sexually aroused. Is this abnormal?"

A. No. Many women have that experience. It merely means that an area of the body especially sensitive to touch has responded to sensual stimulation. Your head may care about what has created that stimulation, but your body couldn't care less!

Q. *"My vagina has gotten so big that my husband complains he can't even 'feel' me, and even I seem to have lost feeling. My mother says that's just the penalty for having babies. Can't something be done?"*

A. Yes, and very easily too. The problem is mainly that the pubococcygal (PC) muscle surrounding part of the vagina has lost its elasticity. Like other muscles it requires exercise to regain and keep its tone. There are three things you can do, and unlike any other exercises you may have done, they require practically no time, effort, or thought:

1) Locate the PC muscle by pretending you're about to urinate, and try to stop the flow *without* using either your legs or buttocks muscles.
2) Tighten the muscle for one or two seconds, then relax it for the same amount of time. Do this exercise in six sessions a day, starting with 10 and working up to a maximum of 50 a session by the end of three weeks.
3) "Twitch" the muscle by contracting and releasing it quickly, starting with 10 and working up to 100 a day.

These exercises can be divided into as many sessions as you wish. They can be done while in bed, washing dishes, stopping the car at a red light, or during a meeting, for they require no thought and are not visible. Try exercising secretly and testing your success by contracting the muscle at some quiet point during intercourse. When your husband wonders if you just did something, you'll know you're on your way, and after that he can help measure the amount of pressure you've exerted.

Not only will these exercises help the sense of "tightness" that men often enjoy, but also they will help increase your feeling, for this reason: the vagina itself has little feeling. Instead, the contraction and relaxation of muscles surrounding the vagina allow sensations from the clitoral area to spread into the vagina, creating the build-up of feelings known as orgasm. Many women report that they can feel a difference within two weeks (or conversely notice a decrease in feeling if they stop exercising for two weeks), and some women have experienced their first orgasm following such exercises.

Q. *"Will intercourse be painful after childbirth?"*

A. Probably not, but many women are understandably apprehensive, and fear alone can create enough tension to cause some discomfort. The man might use both extra gentleness and some added lubrication, such as K-Y Jelly, possibly working toward intercourse gradually over a few nights. If persistent pain occurs, consult your doctor. Occasionally an episiotomy has not healed adequately, and some minor medical correction will help.

Q. *"I still have pain even though the doctors says there's nothing wrong. The more we try, the worse it gets. What should we do?"*

A. Stop trying so hard! Take things in steps, concentrating on relaxing and enjoying pleasurable sensations at each step. Spend a night or two just caressing, and practice inserting your own fingers into your vagina while relaxing your vaginal muscles. When you can do this easily use his fingers (first one and then two) while you practice relaxing. When that is comfortable, practice relaxing while he inserts a little of his penis, using extra lubrication. When (and only when) this is accomplished, try a little more, each time stopping *before* you experience pain. It may require several nights for each step, but *do not attempt to go beyond an agreed-on step in a given session, and do not attempt more than what you are reasonably sure you can achieve.* Many women cannot relax at all if they fear that success at one step will force them into more than they'd planned for that night. So enjoy each small success, and don't worry about the future. If this does not work within a few weeks, seek professional guidance.

Q. *"My wife keeps pleading 'too tired' for sex. Isn't that just an excuse?"*

A. Never underestimate the fatigue of a new mother! It's no excuse—it's real. Anything that can be done to reduce fatigue will help; this includes helping more with chores, reducing work expectations, finding new and more relaxed times for sexual activity, or planning time to be alone and time to sit and relax together, perhaps talking over the day's tensions and having a glass of wine before bedtime. It's tempting to rush to bed frantically trying to beat baby's 2 a.m. feeding, but often some "unwinding" time is more useful.

Q. *"My husband keeps pleading 'too tired' for sex. Isn't that just an excuse?"*

A. Never underestimate the fatigue of a new father! Men, too, can get worn out, distracted, and worried about the responsibilities of parenthood. The earlier comments apply to men too.

Of course "too tired" can cover up fear, anger, or worry for either partner, often related to the tensions of having a new baby. Each partner tries to shoulder his or her burdens alone, either out of misguided attempts to protect the other person or out of fear that his or her thoughts are "wrong" or "abnormal." Another problem is that anyone who is tired is obviously considering sex to be "work" rather than fun and relaxation. Often that happens because people establish preset goals and expectations, and they work so hard to live up to them that they can't possibly enjoy themselves. Because of this, "too tired" often goes hand in hand with any one or all of the following concerns:

"My wife (husband) acts like I'm selfish to want sex, treats it as if it were a 'duty,' and doesn't seem to enjoy it anymore. I feel as if I was just 'used' to get a baby, and now I'm not wanted or needed anymore."

"I feel replaced by the baby. I know it's silly to be jealous, but she won't even let me caress her breasts."

"My breasts are really tender, but I'm afraid to tell him to be more gentle."

"I couldn't get an erection the first time we tried sex, and I was so humiliated that I'm even afraid to kiss her for fear I'll end up failing again."

"He couldn't get an erection, and he never shows me any affection anymore. Have I lost my sex appeal? Doesn't he love me?"

"She doesn't have orgasms and seems to resent any affection I give her. Doesn't she love me anymore?"

"He never acts affectionate unless he wants sex and acts insulted if I don't have an orgasm. I'd be more affectionate, except that it always leads to intercourse, and sometimes I don't want that."

"Sometimes I masturbate when I'm frustrated. Is that all right? My wife (husband) acts like that's an insult, but I don't feel that way."

Underlying these concerns are implicit assumptions that sex means intercourse, and successful sex means orgasm through intercourse, and that anything else implies abnormality, disloyalty, and lack of love. It is these assumptions that turn sex into work and interfere with pleasure and affection. They turn the bedroom into a tense arena for proving one's adequacy, allowing very few ways in which to give or receive pleasure, and creating unrealistic performance expectations that have little to do with one's needs or abilities. Small wonder that so many misinterpretations and resentments occur in a marriage.

Here are some suggestions for resolving such problems:

1) Try thinking of sex not as intercourse but as the giving and receiving of pleasure via the body; you'll see there are many options. Self-stimulation (masturbation) may not be acceptable to all people, but it is one of the quickest and easiest routes to the tension release that orgasm provides. People who have that option are often freed to be more relaxed during intercourse. Kissing, mouth-genital stimulation, manual intercourse (i.e., caressing to orgasm), caressing,

back rubs, and massages are just a few of the other forms of sexual expression. They may or may not lead to intercourse or orgasm yet can be warm, tender, pleasurable, and relaxing all by themselves. A person may find any one of them much more physically satisfying than intercourse itself or might not want intercourse at some point yet be glad to give or receive pleasure in one of these other ways. Not only do individuals vary greatly in their needs and responses, but also they may vary greatly from moment to moment. As long as an activity is acceptable to both partners, there is no "right" or "wrong" way to enjoy sex.

2) Try more honesty about your needs, hopes, and worries. Take time out for a relaxed discussion of how things are going sexually, what outside factors might be interfering, what things you'd enjoy sexually, and what each partner might do to enhance pleasure. (Focus on what you'd like, rather than on what you already dislike, or the experience may become negative instead of positive.)

3) Try a little "motel therapy" along with your discussion. Hire a baby-sitter and go to a motel for a weekend (or even have a sitter take baby out on a long outing), and then try an exercise in sensuality. *Take turns* being a "giver" and a "receiver." In a first session learn to enjoy sex without even touching genitals; in the second learn how to enjoy genital sex without having intercourse; in the third include intercourse along with the sensuality. The "giver" merely strokes or caresses the total body while the "receiver" lies back passively and enjoys it, with no other activity than to possibly guide the giver's hands or to briefly state that a particular activity is not enjoyable. The "giver" should stop whenever boredom sets in, and you should then both discuss your feelings about what you've been doing. You may find that one kind of touch is more enjoyable than another; one area more sensitive; that you may or may not get excited; that erections may come and go; and that physical responses may have changed since childbirth.

You'll learn more about yourselves and each other: that you can have "good" sex without intercourse or even excitement, and that you can each give and get from the relationship. Most important, you will learn that sex is no big thing; if it doesn't turn out quite right one time or one way, it will another time.

Generally, though, if you each use sensitivity, honest communication about your needs, consideration for the other's needs, a bit of humor; if you allow yourselves to both give and receive pleasure in many ways, without striving to reach some preset goal; then sex, no matter what its form, will provide the love and affection, mutual support, and tension release that new parents—perhaps more than most people—badly need. Your lovemaking will then truly take on new meaning and new joy.